Are You BEHIND the Eight Ball?

ISBN: 1463602154
ISBN-13: 9781463602154

ARE YOU BEHIND THE EIGHT BALL?

SIX CORNERSTONES OF FINANCIAL FREEDOM
A PERSONAL FINANCIAL
GUIDE FOR ALL AMERICANS

3rd Edition

By

JACK D. LETZER JR.

Are You BEHIND the Eight Ball?

TABLE OF CONTENTS

OVERVIEW

As I look back on all my years of schooling, consisting primarily of high school and seven years of under-graduate and graduate school education, one issue that clearly stands out is the lack of serious preparation I received with regards to personal financial planning. I was exposed to all the traditional mathematics courses, arts and sciences, history, languages, and other traditional areas of higher education. In college, I majored in Finance and chose that same avenue for my concentration in graduate school. That background prepared me for the corporate world, but any personal financial planning skills were developed largely on my own without any specific guidance. Understanding personal finance is not a casual endeavor requiring only pe-riodic monitoring. It requires a fundamental knowledge of how money works in order to make the proper decisions that will result in the ability to establish credit, buy a home, in-vest in the future and remain debt-free.

We have a looming crisis in our country. Millions of households are not preparing for retirement. They are living to satisfy today's desires by postponing tomorrow's needs. According to the Employee Benefits Research Institute's

2009 Retirement Confidence Survey, the typical American household (headed by a 43 year old), has **only $18,000 in savings!!**[1] That is a shockingly low figure, which indicates, that the typical household has postponed retirement planning for the first two decades out of their working careers and spent too much of their resources on items offering no long term benefits. It shows a complete lack of understanding as to how compound interest rates can generate wealth for one's household. In addition, if these profligate spending habits are continued, these income earners will be forced into working well into their 70s or even their 80s to maintain a quality of life similar to what they enjoy today. If they choose to retire in their mid 60s they will likely be highly dependent on government (social security) to finance their retirement lifestyle. This will undoubtedly result in a significant reduction in standard of living from what they enjoy today, all because they had no foresight and lived for today by borrowing from tomorrow.

Why is an essential life skill such as building a solid financial foundation practically ignored at all levels of schooling? I do not have a clear answer, except to say that it appears that this is one of those skills, similar to maintaining a home, that one is expected to learn by doing. Because of the lack of any proper education in this arena, most people approach personal finance with a great degree of trepidation, opting instead to engage the services of a professional who they hope will take care of their critical financial management needs. People would be wise to remember that no one

---

1   http://20somethingfinance.com/average-retirement-savings/

will look out for their financial well-being with the degree of interest that you will put forth.

The purpose of this book is to assist individuals in maximizing their **net worth,** by improving their personal balance sheets, as well as to provide options for improving their **personal Income Statements** which document their monthly financial performance. A **personal Balance Sheet** *adds* one's household *assets* or possessions, and *subtracts* the total debt balances or *liabilities* to arrive at the individual or household's equivalent net worth. **In essence, what you own less what you owe is what you are worth.** A personal income statement *sums* all the household's monthly sources of income and *subtracts* all associated household monthly living *expenses* to arrive at an equivalent **disposable income or loss** position. While differentiating balance sheets and income statements can be confusing for the individual and may appear to represent issues more relevant to corporate finance and accounting, many of the same principles apply to running your personal finances. The basic difference lies in the fact that a personal income statement is a financial recording **over a period of time,** as to how well a household meets its monthly bills and obligations, given the sources of income at its disposal. A balance sheet is a **snapshot at a specific point in time** which outlines how well the household is doing in terms of increasing its net worth through the increase of its asset base or the decrease of its liabilities. An example of a personal income statement is a monthly household budget, which will be discussed in more detail in the budgeting section of this handbook. A personal balance sheet is included in the beginning of the investment section.

I would not insult the reader's intelligence by pretending to have discovered a silver bullet for wealth creation and I do not counsel individuals on how to "get rich quick." In my opinion, the vast majority of Americans simply want to reach a comfortable financial existence, where they are able to obtain a proper balance between work and their personal lives, save for their family's future, and remain debt free. As the title of the handbook indicates, I will elaborate on six cornerstones of financial success: Building a **B**udget (Personal Income Statement), **E**liminating Debt, **H**ome Ownership, **I**nvesting (the previous three are the key contributors towards Personal Balance Sheet Development), **N**ursing and Long-Term Care Planning, and **D**eath Preparation. The last cornerstone is my euphemism for estate planning and insurance coverage. There will also be a section devoted to the understanding of all tax payments that households are currently subject to, and how to carefully plan around those tax obligations in order to mitigate a painful surprise on April 15.

Financial Planning is **NOT** rocket science. A CPA certification or an **MBA** degree is not required to make what often times are common sense decisions. What is needed is the crucial set of ingredients to success in any field: gaining a fundamental understanding of the critical issues, setting goals, and developing a realistic but challenging plan to meet the goals. In terms of personal finances, this means anticipating major financial hurdles that will occur down the road as well as planning for those events which are currently invisible but could rear their ugly heads at any time.

This book is not meant to provide specific investment guidance or to develop advanced financial skills. It is meant as a tool to enhance financial awareness for any and all demographic groups, with a particular emphasis on young people about to enter the collegiate and working worlds, with respect to the many different facets of personal finance. This guide should **not** be thought of as a replacement of professional financial services. Although I encourage all individuals to be well informed when it comes to managing investments, I would also recommend that individuals seek financial advice when investing in stocks, bonds or mutual funds. Finally, it would also be wise to consult financial and legal professionals in the areas of real estate decision-making, will preparation, insurance coverage, and other specific financial needs.

In this book, we will delve into the six cornerstones of financial freedom by viewing personal financial decisions through the prism of the Smith family. The Smith's are a fictitious household comprising mom, dad and two kids. I will attempt to illustrate key decisions made by the Smith's using some of the personal financial statements we have mentioned. This begins with an understanding of the benefits of budgeting. A budget helps to determine what a household is able to afford with its available disposable income, or the money left over after the monthly bills are paid.

Following is a discussion on the financial stranglehold that significant debt can impose on a family's goals and objectives. We all are aware of anecdotal evidence of individuals who are unable to dig themselves out of a financial hole (eliminating their debt), and many of those lucky enough to do so, invariably achieve that freedom only temporarily and go back into debt.

Subsequent to that, we will review the steps involved in purchasing your own home and understanding all the ancillary costs involved in owning property. Afterwards, we will analyze the global investment landscape with a rudimentary discussion of corporate financial statements and corresponding investment metrics. These will be presented along with other areas of focus including ways in which tax-deferred savings can be used to fund college education. In addition, we will discuss the impact of long-term care and medical costs in general on elderly Americans, as well as the insurance industry in the United States whose purpose it is to provide a means to ensure proper asset protection for your household. We will then discuss principles and benefits of proper estate planning to ensure seamless distribution of a lifetime worth of accumulated assets to your heirs. Finally, we will end our discussion with an overview of the broad tax landscape in the United States and its impact on your household finances.

Before we begin a detailed discussion on the six principles of financial freedom, I believe it is paramount for Americans to have a basic understanding of the macroeconomic environment that surrounds them. For instance, if your household begins the process of purchasing a new home after several years of renting, a looming recession in the domestic economy would significantly affect the decision. You may choose to proceed or defer the purchase, but it would behoove you to have as many facts at your disposal prior to entering into one of the largest financial decisions of your life. Similarly, if you are planning on selling a large block of common stock and the Federal Government is planning on raising capital gains tax rates, your decision to sell could have a serious implication on your finances even though selling the stock might be the right decision for you personally. The point is that a fundamental understanding of the economic environment around you can be just as important to your financial well-being as the intricacies of your particular household.

THE MACROECONOMIC ENVIRONMENT

What is the outlook for the domestic and global economy for the foreseeable future? Such a question typically evokes yawns and blank stares from many people. Every day however, our personal financial situation is increasingly impacted by economic factors outside of our control: gasoline, food and medical bills are just a few of the many types of costs that appear to rise at alarming rates. Unfortunately, these are items that we need for daily living and on a fixed salary, may severely impact one's quality of life as a result. In addition, movie tickets, apparel and airline tickets represent areas of our life that can be considered as "nice to haves" but not essential; yet a steep rise in these will also affect one's quality of life. The universe of economic data is so vast that it can be intimidating to even try to make sense of it. Where do I begin? What does GDP mean? What is the Federal Reserve? Why are interest rates so high for some items and less for others? These are all key questions that directly contribute to your financial well-being. To help answer these, it makes sense to begin with a discussion on interest rates.

WHAT ARE INTEREST RATES?

In their simplest form, interest rates represent the cost of borrowing money[2]. It is the amount you owe the financial institution that provides a particular loan to you for the privilege of using their money, whether it is for an automobile, a student loan, a mortgage or anything else. Since the majority of Americans do not have enough cash on hand to pay for the retail price of a car, a home, an education or most big ticket items, they are forced to "finance" their purchases; meaning, they need to borrow the money and pay it back in periodic installments. These periodic payments (usually monthly) are augmented by the corresponding interest rate charged by the respective financial institution issuing the loan.

For instance, if you buy a car for $20,000, and you pay it back over 5 years, your payment will not equal $20,000 divided by 60 months. That would equal $333.33 per month. In order for the bank to be willing to lend you the money to buy the car, they need to charge a rate of interest on that loan amount that covers their costs of issuing the loan. Since the bank operates a business whose primary purpose is to lend money to consumers, they incur costs in operating that business. If they don't charge the consumer enough money in interest to cover their costs, they will lose money on the transaction. Although most consumers will pay their loan obligations on time, a percentage of them will not and will default on some portion of the loan, potentially resulting in

---

2   http://www.playbook.thehartford.com/servlet/Satellite?c=Page&cid=1107708665428&nt_page_id=1107708665428&pagename=Playbook%2FPage%2FPB_ContentPage

a loss to the bank on that particular loan. Lending institutions need to cover themselves for this risk by ensuring they charge a sufficient rate of interest on all consumer transactions that will offset the loss they will incur on a small percentage of "deadbeat" loans.

Another reason interest rates exist is to allow the bank to recover the "opportunity cost" that they lose by not being able to invest the $20,000 they have lent you to buy the car or use it for another purpose. By definition, they could be investing the same $20,000 at a particular rate of interest and growing that money. By lending you that money over a fixed period of time, they will need to ensure they charge enough in interest to offset the potential gain they would have generated by investing that money. Finally, the interest rate charged to the consumer will allow the bank to generate a reasonable profit since that will allow their business to grow and be in the position to offer more loans to more consumers and possibly provide employment to more individuals. Automobile loans in 2008 are issued with interest rates that range in the low single digits for most consumers. If we assume a 4% interest rate on the $20,000 loan and 5 years to pay back the loan, you can expect to pay approximately $367 per month for that loan. That equates to a total of $22,020 you will pay for the car over the life of the loan. The extra $2,020 represents the amount the bank will earn in interest to cover their operating costs, their opportunity costs and their profit on the loan.

The amount of interest that is charged for a particular loan depends on many factors. For instance, interest rates on car loans and student loans for the average consumer are typically substantially lower than interest rates on loans for credit cards and personal loans. A key reason for this is that if the consumer defaults on a car loan, the institution issuing the loan can repossess the vehicle. That is the "collateral" for the loan, which in essence is what the consumer pledges as repayment to the financial institution in case that person defaults on the loan payment. This is an example of **secured debt**. With respect to student loans, average interest rates also are usually lower than other loan types. These loans often times are subsidized by Federal, State or Local Governments, which result in lower interest rates than might otherwise be the case. Anecdotal evidence also indicates that since students are investing in their educations, they historically have a better track record of payments on these loans, justifying lower rates.

Credit card loan interest rates on the other hand, are typically among the highest in the industry. The reason for this is that like personal loans, the lending institution has little to no assets from the borrower that they can claim as collateral. This is also referred to as **unsecured** debt. Therefore, if the borrower defaults, the lending institution has little to no recourse to recover their money. As a result, credit card companies charge very high interest rates, often into the mid-twenty percent range. This allows the credit card company to pass along the costs of borrowers who default onto borrowers who do repay their loans. The key for financially savvy consumers is to use credit cards sparingly and repay any outstanding amount by the end of each billing cycle in order to avoid interest charges.

HOW ARE INTEREST RATES SET? WHAT IS MONETARY POLICY?

Did you ever wonder just how interest rates are set? How is it that 5 year car loans can have interest rates in the low - mid single digits while 30 year mortgage rates can have similar interest rates? Or how is it that 1 year credit card interest rates can have interest rates in the 15% - 25% range but 10 year student loan rates can hover at rates that are 1/3 of that amount? To begin to understand these differences it is important to understand the basics of the "yield curve".

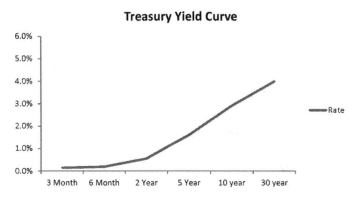

http://www.yieldcurve.com/marketyieldcurve.asp

The yield curve (typically refers to US Treasury securities) reflects the relationship between interest rates for fixed income securities (think bonds) and their time to maturity. Typically, it covers the periods of 3 months to 30 years. The interest rates are divided into short term (less than one year) and long term (more than one year) rates. In a normal or upward sloping yield curve, short term rates (yields) are less than long term rates because of the perceived risk involved with holding long term debt securities. In essence, the longer you hold debt (own bonds) the greater the interest rate risk the lender assumes, that they will not receive the amount invested (principal) + the investment premium (interest) they were promised. That is why investors typically require a higher return on long term debt instruments compared to short term debt instruments. **It is to make up for the additional default risk and the time value of money associated with longer holding periods**.

Short term rates (< 1 year) are controlled by the Federal Reserve (The Fed), a group of quasi-government banks who have among their respective charters the responsibility of controlling the money supply and the amount of credit available in the US economy. Long term rates are driven by market forces dictated primarily by supply and demand for goods and services.

The Federal Reserve banks (there are 12 geographically dispersed throughout the US) strive to achieve their charter or implement the requisite *monetary policy* in order to achieve the following objectives[3]:

- Promote sustainable growth in the economy to achieve high / full employment levels
- Promote price stability

And:

- Preserve the purchasing power for the US Dollar (while not an official mandate, it certainly is a goal

---

3   www.federalreserve.gov/pf/pdf/pf_2.pdf

for the Fed made possible by achieving the first two goals)

They achieve these objectives by taking one or a combination of all of the following actions:

- Buying and selling Government securities (a.k.a "open market operations")
- Increasing or decreasing the discount rate and / or federal funds rate
- Increasing or decreasing the "required reserves" of commercial banks throughout the country.

WHAT DOES ANY OF THIS HAVE TO DO WITH MANAGING MY FINANCES?

Believe it or not, these few bullets will directly impact your personal finances throughout your life. Take the first objective: *promoting sustainable growth*. This means the Federal Reserve will take whatever steps are necessary and within their control to keep the economy growing at a "reasonable" rate and in turn drive unemployment levels down as much as possible without hurting the economy.

WHY WOULDN'T THE FED WANT THE ECONOMY TO GROW AS FAST AS POSSIBLE?

The size of the US economy is measured by the quarterly GDP report. **GDP stands for Gross Domestic Product and is the aggregate value of all goods and services produced in a given period of time in the US economy.** This value is compared to the GDP for the same period one year previous in order to measure the growth in the economy during the same period. If the economy grows at an accelerated or unsustainable pace, *inflation* will likely take hold, which in the long run will stifle economic growth.

2009 GDP Rankings by Nation (USD)

United States	14.0 Trillion
Japan	5.0 Trillion
China	4.8 Trillion
Germany	3.1 Trillion
France	2.5 Trillion
United Kingdom	2.0 Trillion
Italy	2.0 Trillion
Spain	1.4 Trillion
Brazil	1.3 Trillion
Canada	1.2 Trillion
India	1.2 Trillion
Russia	1.2 Trillion
Mexico	.8 Trillion
Australia	.8 Trillion
Netherlands	.7 Trillion
South Korea	.7 Trillion
Turkey	.6 Trillion
Indonesia	.5 Trillion
Switzerland	.5 Trillion
Belgium	.4 Trillion

http://www.suite101.com/content/
gdp-estimates-for-richest-countries-in-2009-a127486

As you can see by the ranking of greatest GDP producers worldwide, the United States has by far the greatest economic engine of any single country in the world. It helps that ~300 million inhabitants contribute to this ranking, but never-the-less, Japan , at ~$5.0 Trillion, is the closest single country rival producing just over 1/3 the amount. The purpose of this table is to place the US economy in context: for all of its critics and shortcomings, the US capitalist system is a juggernaut and is a major force driving the global economy. Monetary and Fiscal policy decisions can and will greatly impact the growth in the economy.

This brings us to our second objective: *the promotion of price stability*. Inflation in an economic sense is a condition in which "too much money is chasing too few goods" manifested by a general increase in the price level for a basket of goods in the economy. When the economy becomes "overheated" the value of your cash on hand and your assets in general will cheapen. Another way to think about this is that under inflationary conditions, it takes more and more money to buy the same set of goods.

HOW DO WE KNOW IF WE HAVE INFLATION AND HOW COULD THIS AFFECT ME?

There are two economic metrics regularly used to measure the rate of inflation. These are the:

- Consumer Price Index (CPI)
- Producer Price Index (PPI)

These indices are published monthly. The CPI attempts to measure the overall increase in prices of a basket of goods at the consumer level (i.e., food & beverage, housing, apparel, transportation, etc.). In 2008 most Americans were affected by the dramatic increase in gas and food prices. In 2006, gasoline prices were as low as $2 per gallon but in less than 24 months prices at the retail (consumer) level spiked to over $4 per gallon before coming back down; that is a gain of 100% in just 2 years!! Food prices also rose significantly during that period. For instance, corn, milk and other staples experienced dramatic price rises during this time. Price increases are due to a variety of reasons but the proximate cause for them is driven by **supply and demand** factors.

Although this is not an Economics book, it pays to have a rudimentary knowledge of supply and demand. For argument's sake let's use gasoline for this discussion. Theoretically, as consumer demand for gasoline rises as typically occurs during the summer driving season, supplies of gasoline are expected to climb in a similar fashion in order to keep the price relatively stable. If supplies do not increase in a corresponding manner, the price of gasoline will continue to increase because it is deemed to be that much more valuable to the public who wants it, since it is now in shorter supply. The continued increase in price should eventually attract more suppliers of gasoline or substitute products because they will perceive that there is a significant profit or gain to be made by producing and selling more of those products. Eventually as greater supplies of gasoline or alternative products begin to make their way into the marketplace, the price will come back down to a point of equilibrium where market forces now perceive supply and demand factors to be in balance. This theory works exactly in the reverse fashion as well with decreasing supplies of a good or service if demand for such is perceived to be decreasing.

One final note on the CPI: since the prices of food and energy are so volatile and can be affected by seasonal factors as well, the CPI is typically reported in two ways: the Core CPI rate excludes food and energy and the Total CPI rate includes food and energy costs.

Like consumer prices, the PPI also measures the increase or decrease in a basket of prices to be paid by producers. Producers typically need to purchase raw materials (petroleum, aluminum, copper, soybeans, oranges, etc…) in order to convert them to finished goods for the consuming public (gasoline, building siding, construction piping, food, orange juice, etc…). The prices paid by producers are closely tracked by the PPI in order to determine if inflationary pressures are apparent in the economy.

Our last major Fed objective relates to *maintaining the purchasing power of the US dollar*. In essence, purchasing power measures whether a specific amount of the currency is able to buy the same amounts of goods and services it used to be able to purchase in the global economy. The price of oil is a perfect example. Throughout much of the first decade of the 21st century, the US Dollar weakened in value against major currencies worldwide for a variety of reasons, some of which are intentional on the part of the US Government. As a result, petroleum, which is priced in "dollars per barrel" in the global economy, has seen its cost to the consumer rise very steeply over a relatively short period of time. This is **not** to say that the price of oil has risen **only** because the value of the dollar has weakened. It is but one contributing factor. The major reason is that demand has soared worldwide relative to the current level of supply in the marketplace, as developing nations like China and India generate substantial growth in their economies as they begin to adopt free market principles.

As mentioned, the US Dollar weakened significantly against most major currencies throughout the world. In the early part of the decade, the USD and the Euro were at parity, meaning 1 USD = 1 Euro. As of November 2010, 1.35 USD = 1 Euro, meaning that over the course of several years, the USD has depreciated by 35% against the Euro. In other words, the value of the dollar shrunk so much that 35% more dollars were required to purchase what 1 USD used to purchase only several years prior. At a personal level this significantly impacts Americans traveling overseas and households wishing to purchase imported goods and services. For those wondering if this relationship affects only trade with European nations, consider the USD / Japanese Yen relationship. In the same time frame, the Yen has appreciated against the USD by ~38%, trading today at ~83 Yen / USD, whereas in the early part of the decade, each USD commanded as much as 135 Yen.

WHY DID THIS HAPPEN?
This is a matter of great debate and several reasons exist. We will discuss some of these in more detail. First, some of

the dollar weakness has in the past been intentional. The US Government for some time has believed that the US needs to increase its exports of goods and services to other countries in order to reduce the nation's trade deficit. Makers of heavy equipment such as Deere and Caterpillar benefited from this situation. In addition, global software services giants like IBM and Microsoft also benefited from the dollar weakness as their sales overseas increased significantly.

Second, the US maintains an annual trade deficit, which is a negative trade balance. The trade deficit is the difference between the goods and services Americans sell to foreigners and the goods and services that Americans purchase from foreigners[4]. This figure approximated $44 billion for the month of September 2010 which means that on an annual basis the total annual trade deficit was projected to range between $500B - $600B. Even though the US saw its aggregate exports rise over the last several years and contributed to a strong US economy from 2003 – 2007 (in terms of GDP growth), as a nation we continue to purchase significantly more foreign goods than we sell driving the trade deficit ever higher. The concern with a protracted trade deficit is that the longer we continue to send more of our currency overseas, we are placing our economic future in the hands of foreign countries (i.e.; China). If these foreign countries / governments lack long-term confidence in the US economy they may "sell" their dollar holdings on the open market in exchange for other currencies they consider more valuable. This would increase the supply of dollars in the marketplace, and in turn weaken the currency relative to other major nations of the world.

---

4   http://www.americaneconomicalert.org/ticker_home.asp

Third, the US has run budget deficits for many years. A budget deficit is the net difference between total government tax revenues and total government spending. A deficit means the government spends more than it takes in. The official figure for 2009 was in excess of $1.4 Trillion!!! What a staggering figure. Note that this included the federal government's approved bailout of the financial industry (we will discuss the Subprime Mortgage scandal later in this handbook) at the end of 2008 which added ~$700B - $750B in *deficit* spending. When the government runs a budget deficit, which it has done almost every year since 1969, it needs to borrow the difference in the form of bonds issued to individuals, corporations and foreign governments, which incur interest charges on top of the principal borrowed. This in turn drives up the total National Debt to levels that as of 2010 exceed *$14 Trillion*. The National Debt is the accumulation of all budget deficits, and in 2010 is basically equal to the size of the entire US economy. Another way to say this is that the National Debt now equals GDP!!!

Similar to the US trade deficit, if we as a nation, continue squandering our country's total tax receipts by spending significantly more than we collect in revenue, the end result will be the continued devaluation of the USD, soaring interest rates to ward off accelerated inflation and possibly plunging the economy into a deep recession with unacceptable rates of unemployment.

The previous two reasons for USD weakness are direct examples of the US Government squandering taxpayer dollars. The last reason is our own fault as a society. As a nation,

Americans save much less than we used to. In recent times, we have been a debtor nation both at a personal level and at a Government level. As recently as the mid-1980's, our nation saved approximately 10% of total annual income in terms of total GDP. In 2005 conversely, as a nation we actually spent more than we made and had a savings rate of negative .5%. In 2010, primarily due to the sub-prime mortgage crisis, we have begun saving again to some extent, recording a personal savings rate of ~ 6%. [5] This rebound in the savings rate can be attributed to the recent sub-prime mortgage crisis which we will address shortly.

What changed? I believe that over the last 2-3 decades, our society has increasingly sought instant gratification and demands a certain quality of life today that previous generations used to patiently save for many years before they could enjoy that same quality of life. As a result, we purchase items that we don't really own using credit cards, but have been given access to these items as long as we continue paying the credit card debt over time. This can be another contributing factor towards a weaker USD, because increased consumption of goods and services can lead to a flooding of currency in the marketplace; if this greater supply of dollars chases lesser demand for those dollars, it will drive down the value of the currency.

As you can see, major price fluctuations (particularly with food and petroleum), a weakening USD and decreasing growth in the overall economy are a major focus for the

---

5   http://money.cnn.com/2010/08/03/news/economy/personal_income_spending/index.htm

Federal Reserve. The skyrocketing price of gasoline in 2007-2008 turned a theoretical discussion on the role of the Fed into a real life situation that affected every American's personal finances. What can the Fed do to respond to this and other economic situations given its overall monetary policy mandate?

The Fed will typically take a holistic or macro view of the economy and not set policy based on individual or isolated situations. As such, if it determines that inflationary pressures exist and they threaten to undermine economic growth, resulting in increasing levels of unemployment and price instability as well as potentially harming the value of the currency, they are expected to act to address the needs of that particular circumstance.

If the Fed believes the Government is growing at an unsustainable rate, and that inflation is imminent, they may choose to slow the economy down in a gradual manner, hopefully mitigating inflation and at the same time working to avoid a **recession** should they slow the economy down too rapidly. A recession is an economic condition manifested by the contraction of the domestic economy, historically measured as two successive quarters of year over year reductions in GDP. The Fed can begin to slow the economy down to mitigate inflationary pressures in any or all of the following manners:

1. They may choose to sell Treasury securities to banks via "open market operations", thereby draining reserves from the banking system and placing those

funds out of circulation. By reducing the money supply, the Fed works to increase the value of the currency remaining in circulation. Conversely, if the Fed believes the economy is slowing down too fast, resulting in recessionary pressures to the economy, they may choose to purchase Treasury securities from banks, adding currency to the banking system, which would result in the immediate infusion of money supply into the marketplace. This gets more money in circulation with the goal of "kick-starting" the economy.

2. Second, the Fed can exercise its monetary policy by altering the short term interest rate environment. Remember our yield curve. The Fed can alter the short term interest rate environment with the hopes of stimulating or decelerating economic growth and directly affect long term interest rates such as mortgage rates. If they believe economic conditions are such that GDP is *accelerating* too rapidly, they can *raise* either of the following:

   • Discount Rate (Discount window) – this is the rate at which the Fed will lend money to commercial banks. Banks need to have a certain amount of cash reserves on hand to meet reserve requirements, short term financing needs, etc... If a particular bank faces short term liquidity needs, they have the option of going directly to their regional Federal Reserve branch to ask for a short term loan at the *Discount Rate* (a.k.a lender of last resort) in order to meet their liquidity needs. Banks often will pass on this option since borrowing from the Fed exposes a bank to many unwanted bureaucratic questions which can be more of a hassle than they are worth.

- Federal Funds Rate – this is also known as the "overnight lending rate" and it is the rate at which banks can borrow from one another in order to meet their reserve requirements, and other short term liquidity needs. This is a much more palatable option for banks and although it usually is a slightly higher rate than the discount rate, banks prefer this option as it avoids what they deem to be unnecessary regulatory hassles.

During an expansionary period (accelerating economy), the Fed may opt to raise one or both of these interest rates multiple times over the course of several months. The desired objective will be to slow the economy down because borrowers will eventually choose not to borrow money at increasing levels of interest. During periods of economic **slowdown**, the Fed may choose to **decrease** one or both of these rates multiple times in order to **stimulate** borrowing by corporations and consumers, and in turn "revving up" the economy since inflationary pressures will be deemed to be contained. The Fed would then be moving to avert an economic recession which would likely result in higher levels of unemployment, with little to no growth in the overall economy.

The other key weapon in the Fed's arsenal is the setting of required reserves for commercial banks. As mentioned previously, banks are required to have a minimum amount of cash and or other reserves on hand. This minimum is set as a percentage of the total amount of customer deposits in the bank, and is designed to ensure that banks will have adequate reserves to handle normal daily business. This minimum percentage is called the **required reserve ratio** (because it expresses the requirement as a percentage of total customer deposits). Of course, a bank can keep reserves in excess of the minimum required. These are known as **excess reserves**.

If the Fed believes the economy is beginning to accelerate and grow at a rate that could become unsustainable, meaning that inflationary pressures are expected to increase, the Fed can direct banks to increase their required reserves and make less money available for borrowing by the public. This will contribute to a gradual slowdown in the economy by placing less money in circulation. Conversely, if the Fed believes the economy is beginning to slow down resulting in recessionary fears, the Fed can guide banks to decrease the required reserve ratio, allowing for an easier credit policy to take hold, hopefully spurring the economy and "priming the pump" so to speak.[6]

SO WHAT DOES ALL THIS MEAN TO ME?

Now that we know how *short* term interest rates are set, their effect ripples throughout the rest of the economy, as all other interest rates affecting consumers follow the Fed's lead (individuals and companies are not able to borrow directly from the Fed). For instance, two of the key rates are

6   http://en.wikipedia.org/wiki/Reserve_requirement

the Prime Rate and LIBOR (London Inter-Bank Offer Rate). These are rates on consumer loans that banks use to lend to their best customers who tend to be larger corporations and commercial businesses. As a result, many other commercial loans to smaller businesses may be priced at rates which are based on either of these two benchmarks, such as Prime + 1%, Prime + 2%, etc... The extra percentages on top of the prime rate allow the banks to recover what they believe to be additional risk they are undertaking in lending money to customers not deemed to be of stellar credit.

If the Fed believes the economy is slowing down and recessionary pressures are taking hold which may increase unemployment rates, they may choose to lower the Discount Rate and / or the Federal Funds rates, often (but certainly not always) in ¼ % increments. The ripple effect takes place as banks will quickly follow the Fed's lead and raise or lower their key lending rates to customers. If rates are reduced it provides consumers with greater incentives to borrow since the total cost of borrowing will have been reduced. This spurs economic activity and if rates are lowered sufficiently will eventually introduce inflationary pressures through the injection of a much greater supply of money into the economy.

I mentioned at the outset of this chapter that the Fed sets short term rates and that long term rates are set primarily by market forces based on supply and demand fundamentals. Student loan rates, automobile loan rates and mortgage rates represent three classic examples of longer term interest rates which influence and are influenced by the activity of the

Fed on the short end of the yield curve. Although this can be confusing, it is important to understand that the Fed reacts to long term supply and demand fundamentals to provide them guidance on their interest rate manipulation activities. Once the Fed takes action it is their hope that the long end of the yield curve (long term rates) will move in a particular direction based on the monetary policy they implement.

As an example, if the economy is slowing down, you will see long term interest rates coming down. The reason for this is the marketplace is indicating that the cost of borrowing for commercial loans, mortgages, cars, and big-ticket purchases that credit cards are used for, are too expensive and is discouraging economic activity. One key long term interest rate that the Fed focuses on very closely is the average mortgage rate nationwide. Mortgage rates typically track the 10 year US Treasury note. They rise and fall depending on supply and demand factors in the economy. From 2000 – 2006, the housing industry in the United States experienced an incredible increase in home values, rising as much as 130% on average (including inflation) over those six years.[7] It was as much of a "seller's market" as any period in decades in which buyer's were bidding up the value of homes on the market at a fever pitch. An environment of low mortgage rates and excess money supply in the economy fueled what in retrospect appears to have been a housing "bubble" with property values rising astronomically, and in turn pricing many new entrants out of the market.

---

7   http://designandgeography.com/2011/04/27/housing-price-index-for-the-united-states-2000-2010/

From 2006 - 2008, housing values plummeted across the nation (15% - 25% on average depending on different regions;) as demand for new and existing homes decreased significantly at the same time that an over-abundance of supply hit the market. Homes that typically saw several purchase contracts the same day that they came on the market during the "bubble" period, sat on the market for weeks and months after the "bubble" burst in late 2006, before attracting any purchase bids. What happened? Numerous factors contributed to this fall, but prominent among them is the sub-prime mortgage crisis. Keep in mind that property values (prices) had risen so sharply that all the market needed was some key event to serve as a catalyst to reverse this excessive increase in values.

During economic boom times you will always have excesses in the economy. The sub-prime mortgage crisis is just one example of this. Sub-prime loans are loans made to consumers with inferior credit scores. Since average housing prices had risen so steeply in the previous 3-5 years (historically, home prices rise 5% - 6% annually), many lenders became complacent and believed they could ease their lending standards and begin offering larger and larger loans to clients who posed increased odds of default. This increased lending was coupled with strong federal government urging of banks to augment their mortgage loan portfolios to disadvantaged communities[8].

---

8   http://www.subprimemortgageplan.com/Community_
     Reinvestment_Act_Subprime_Mortgage_Crisis.php

As a result, many mortgage loans were issued to clients who required little to no down-payment, and allowed these prospective homeowners to lock in their mortgage loans with very low interest rates for the first few years of the loan period. However, unbeknownst to many subprime borrowers, these low interest rates (teaser rates) were still tied to the prevailing interest rates in the market. When interest rates (both short and long) began climbing in 2006 and 2007, they triggered significant increases in these **variable** interest rate loans (discussed in more detail in the Home Ownership chapter) whose movements closely tracked the movements of the 10 Year US Treasury Bond rate.

Once these variable mortgage interest rates began their climb (variable rates are fixed for a specific period and then vary according to market forces), they added as much as several hundred dollars per month to a typical mortgage payment for many of these sub-prime borrowers. Long term mortgage rates, although still lower than shorter term rates at the time, began to increase, due in large measure to an excess of money supply in the economy from government efforts to ensure there was enough liquidity in the economy to fuel the demand for homes. This excess money supply (a.k.a. (cheap money") eventually triggered inflationary pressures in the economy[9] manifested by steep price increases at the consumer and producer levels. The market then tried to curb these inflationary pressures through higher interest rates, which act as a disincentive to borrow, hopefully resulting in a reduction in the money supply.

---

9   http://www.reuters.com/article/idUSN1661218020080116

Many sub-prime borrowers were unable to meet these steeper monthly payments which led many of them to default on their payments. As defaults increased, so did foreclosures in which case the bank repossessed the property from the individual. As the rate of homes in the foreclosure process began to climb (2% of residential properties were in foreclosure in 2009),[10] many financial institutions issuing these loans began reporting steep losses as their exposure to these loans was significant.

In mid 2007, the Fed began to see the rate of foreclosures climb and realized that if they did not act quickly, the effects of this housing crisis could and would spread to other parts of the economy severely impacting banks and other financial institutions. This crisis had the potential to negatively impact the growth of the economy and bring about a recession. As far back as 2006, The Fed began to see that the long term rates in the yield curve were lower than the short term rates. This phenomenon is known as an "inverted" yield curve and it can presage a recession in the economy because it tells investors that the costs of borrowing in the short term are too high and are curbing investment activity in the economy.

Throughout the second half of 2007, once the Fed realized that the sub-prime mortgage crisis could drag down the whole economy, they went on a campaign to lower short term rates precipitously in order to "kick start" the slowing economy. Despite extraordinary efforts, the Fed was unable to mitigate the recessionary impact fueled by the sub-prime mortgage crisis due to a whole host of factors. By 2008, short

---

10   http://money.cnn.com/2010/01/14/real_estate/record_foreclosure_year/

term interest rates approached 0%, housing activity had col-
lapsed with respect to new and existing home sales, many
banks had declared bankruptcy in the process, and vener-
able financial institutions such as Lehman Brothers, Merrill
Lynch, AIG, Fannie Mae and Freddie Mac, had either gone
out of business or were forced to merge with other companies due to their exposure to sub-prime mortgage loans
which wound up infecting their enormous asset portfolios.

The sub-prime mortgage crisis will take a long time
to unravel and there are many culprits: consumers for rushing to purchase homes they couldn't afford; predatory lenders for issuing loans they knew certain consumers would be
unable to pay back, just so they could pocket hefty commissions; government for pushing financial institutions to
issue more and more loans in the sub-prime market; Fannie
Mae and Freddie Mac (quasi-government agencies who guaranteed the fiscal soundness of these mortgages) for corrupt
activities and not sounding the alarm that these mortgages
threatened to negatively affect the whole economy; and Wall
Street institutions for failing to implement strict oversight
and "due diligence" over the massive purchases they were
making of these toxic loans under the guise that they were
safe investments.

Understand that our capitalist system by its very nature
has "boom" and "bust" cycles which self-regulate its activities. Recessions will always occur to curb the excesses of
protracted periods of growth. Had the sub-prime mortgage
affair never taken place, something else would have eventually occurred that would have triggered significant rises

in asset values (stocks, bonds, real estate) that would have required the market to self-correct, and enter into a recession, requiring both the Fed and the Congress / President to take actions they believe were necessary to keep the economy on sound footing.

WHAT IS FISCAL POLICY?

As the Fed implements its monetary policy and focuses on all the relevant economic movements, the Federal, State and Local Governments do NOT sit idly by. Fiscal policy is the means by which a government adjusts its levels of spending and taxation in order to influence the nation's economy.[11] Governments at all levels maintain budgets that are driven by revenues (tax collections) and expenditures (spending programs). Prior to the Great Depression, the Federal Government adopted a *laissez faire* approach to the economy, where it allowed the marketplace to dictate economic activity and to regulate itself. After World War II, the government believed it had a duty to reduce unemployment levels and reduce some of the volatility in the traditional business cycles and interest rate movements within the economy.

Similar to the Fed, and depending on the level of economic activity, the government may choose to adopt an **expansionary** or a **contractionary** posture: expansionary policies are those meant to grow the economy while "contractionary" policies aim to slow down the economy to prevent accelerated inflation from taking hold. The government may implement expansionary measures in one of the

---

11   http://www.investopedia.com/articles/04/051904.asp

following ways: first, they can reduce one or more of the many different tax rates they control (this will be discussed in more detail in the tax chapter toward the end of the book). In addition, they can adjust the levels of expenditures made into the economy so as to influence economic activity. For instance, if the Federal Reserve indicates that the level of economic activity is slowing to the point that a recession is a probability, the government will likely implement policies that encourage spending levels to rise in the economy, with the goal of stimulating economic activity.

WHAT DOES THE GOVERNMENT LOOK FOR TO INDICATE A RECESSION IS LOOMING?

We mentioned previously that GDP is the aggregate sum of all goods and services produced by the economy over a given period. If Corporate America begins to create fewer and fewer new jobs every month, or even suffers a net loss of jobs over a given period of time, unemployment levels will begin to rise. If unemployment levels begin to rise, chances are that consumers will begin to restrain their spending levels which will cause a ripple effect in the overall economy. Should this occur, economic growth will become muted or actually begin to contract, possibly leading to a recession. Should these events slowly begin to materialize, the government could draft legislation that would stimulate economic activity. One way to do this would be to decrease tax rates for consumers and / or corporations in one or more of the following areas:

- Income – taxes on gross salaries for *individuals* and net profit for *corporations*

- Payroll – taxes on gross salaries less tax deferred savings and medical accounts used to fund Social Security and Medicare (a.k.a FICA)
  - Applies to both employees and employers at an equivalent percentage rate (7.65%)
- Capital Gains –taxes on profits in investments in stocks, bonds, real estate, etc...

The effect of decreasing one or more of these taxes would be to encourage private investment and spending in the broader economy, because consumers and corporations would have a greater degree of income at their disposal. With this extra income, individuals could purchase new goods that would serve to energize the economy. They could also choose to save for a child's education or to fund a daughter's wedding. Companies of all sizes could use the extra income to hire additional personnel or invest in equipment that would allow them to expand their businesses. In essence, more money in the pockets of consumers and / or corporations stimulates many different types of economic activities which in turn decrease unemployment levels and help the country's GDP to expand.

In addition to decreasing income, capital gain or payroll tax rates, the government (Federal, State or Local) has the ability to inject money into the economy in other ways. Similar to the Fed's ability to control the money supply, the government can choose to increase fiscal spending in large projects meant to drive up employment levels. These could include highway construction projects, public works initiatives, military spending increases for national security purposes, etc… Like tax decreases, these actions would spur increased levels of economic activity which are expansionary in nature. **The problem with fiscal spending is that the government has a long history of spending exorbitant amounts of taxpayer dollars on areas offering little to no return for the overall economy.** Some of these are known as "pork-barrel" projects and are often done to pander to the constituency of individual Congressmen or women, with the hopes of being re-elected by being perceived as being "in touch" with the needs of the local community.

Should the government decide to exercise its prerogative to decrease one or more taxes and / or increase spending, the direct result would be to significantly increase the money supply in the economy. As we discussed in the monetary policy overview, the combination of these actions would probably increase the odds of inflation taking hold in the economy, which would eventually increase the price of goods and services and decrease the purchasing power of the currency you hold. In addition, with additional fiscal spending, it is very likely that the Government will spend more than it takes in tax collections, creating a **budget deficit**.

Budget deficits (both at the Federal and State & Local levels) occur when the Government spends more money than it takes in. This usually is a result of poor fiscal discipline. In addition, this is may be a contributing factor in weakening the value of the currency because deficits typically result in excess money supply in the system, increasing inflationary pressures and cheapening the value of your personal assets and the USD. If the Government spends in excess of its collections, it must borrow or print the shortfall, which increases its total debt load forcing it to pay back interest on the debt as well as the principal amount borrowed. When budget deficits occur in multiple years, you get an accumulation of debt. This is known as the **national debt**.[12]

Sometimes, the Government decides to increase one or more taxes (it has many different tax options at its disposal which will be discussed further at the end of this book) previously discussed in order to reign in the deficit. This does tend to increase revenues in the short term. The problem is that tax hikes can lead to a contraction of the economy, as more money is taken out of the private sector. This money then becomes unavailable for risk takers to use to invest those funds in additional hiring or for large capital projects, which is how our economy traditionally expands.

The Federal Government in 2009 generated gross revenues from all tax collections of $2.1 Trillion!!! This figure was lower than the record of $2.6 Trillion set in 2007 due in large measure to the recession that began in late 2007, but still represents a massive amount of tax revenue. The problem is that the government spent ~$3.5 Trillion[13], resulting in a budget deficit of approximately $1.4 Trillion. The cumulative national debt in turn now exceeds $14 Trillion!![14] Approximately half of the 2009 deficit was due to a poorly executed fiscal stimulus plan implemented by the Obama Administration. The goal of this stimulus plan was to inject

---

12   http://www.investorwords.com/3200/National_Debt.html

13   http://www.usgovernmentrevenue.com/yearrev2009_0.html

14   http://www.usdebtclock.org/

massive amounts of money into the economy with the goal of kick-starting economic activity and lowering unemployment; however, those objectives were not achieved, leaving the government with massive amounts of red ink and an economy on the brink of a second recession in three years.

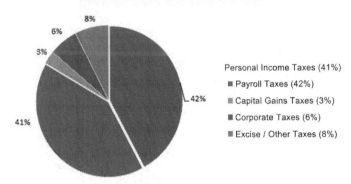

2009 Federal Tax Revenue (~$2.1T)

Personal Income Taxes (41%)
■ Payroll Taxes (42%)
■ Capital Gains Taxes (3%)
■ Corporate Taxes (6%)
■ Excise / Other Taxes (8%)

www.usgovernmentrevenue.com/yearrev2009_0.html

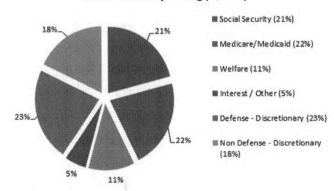

2009 Federal Spending (~$3.5T)

■ Social Security (21%)
■ Medicare/Medicaid (22%)
■ Welfare (11%)
■ Interest / Other (5%)
■ Defense - Discretionary (23%)
■ Non Defense - Discretionary (18%)

www.usgovernmentspending.com/yearrev2009_0.html

Although $1.4 Trillion in deficit is a staggering figure, historically, government deficits have not directly led to the destabilization of the economy. Eventually though, unless great strides are taken to reduce significant annual budget deficits, the impact to the economy may be extremely severe. This could mean significant recessions causing unemployment figures nationwide to increase from their present level of 9.8%. One possible reason that total government debt has not had a more detrimental impact on the economy is that total GDP in 2009 was approximately $14 Trillion. This is by far the largest of any nation which no other country even approaches. When the US has run deficits in the past, they have typically ranged from 1% - 4% of GDP, which in that context, represents a manageable debt level in the eyes of most economists. In 2009, the deficit reached 10% of GDP, a figure we last reached in WWII.

This relatively small budget deficit ratio to the size of the total US economy should not provide solace to Congress. They remain profligate spenders who jeopardize our collective economic security. As we saw in 2009 with the fallout of the sub-prime mortgage fallout and the bailouts of the financial, automotive and insurance industries, the federal government ratcheted up spending to unsustainable levels. In 2009, the Federal budget deficit as a % of GDP reached ~10%, and in 2010, it will likely reach 11% of GDP, as the Obama Administration continues their push to make the federal government the engine of economic recovery.

HOW DOES THE GOVERNMENT SPEND US TAXPAYER DOLLARS?

Like any corporation or household, the Federal Government has an income stream and it incurs costs in running its operations. Virtually all of the government's income is represented by tax collections from individuals, corporations and payroll taxes[15]. Government spending is segregated into two key categories, *Discretionary and Non-Discretionary* spending.

Non-discretionary spending by definition consists of government expenditures deemed mandatory. This would include expenditures covering areas such as Medicare, Social Security, Medicaid, and Welfare. These are also referred to as "entitlements" because recipients receive benefits based on their age, income or other criteria. An additional key area of mandatory spending covers *interest owed on the national debt*. In a typical year, **non-discretionary (mandatory) spending is equivalent to approximately 2/3 of the annual Federal budget**[16]. In 2009, total Federal spending reached $3.52 Trillion, about $2.1 Trillion of which was spent on items Americans **cannot or do not have the will to reduce spending**. Since the aggregate revenues for the USG reached only$2.1 Trillion, mandatory spending accounted for *100%* of revenues, meaning that all discretionary spending had to be paid for by borrowing funds!![17]

---

15   http://www.taxpolicycenter.org/briefing-book/background/
numbers/revenue.cfm

16   http://nationalpriorities.org/resources/federal-budget-101/budget-
briefs/federal-discretionary-and-mandatory-spending/

17   http://www.usgovernmentspending.com/year2009_0.html

What makes this type of spending mandatory? What would happen if we reduced these expenses (except for the interest on the accumulated debt), substantially? The political reality is that since these expenses reflect promises and guarantees made to many citizens over the years (going back to 1935 for Social Security and 1965 for Medicare), any material reduction in these expenses would be deemed suicidal for those Congressmen and Senators who would propose them. Unfortunately, the government has so mismanaged the Social Security and Medicare programs that current statistics indicate that both programs will be insolvent within a couple of decades unless major structural reform is undertaken.

WHAT ARE SOCIAL SECURITY AND MEDICARE?

In the immediate aftermath of the Great Depression which was spawned by the Stock Market Crash of 1929, millions of Americans were left with little to no income, and many senior citizens had virtually no savings to support their retirement. As a result, FDR signed the Social Security Act in 1935, a social insurance program funded through dedicated **payroll taxes** on every American's taxable salary and is known as the Federal Insurance Contributions Act (FICA)[18]. It is also recognized under the acronym OASDI (Old Age Survivors and Disability Income). The tax is currently 6.2% of one's taxable salary (4.2% for 2010 and 2011) matched by another 6.2% that the employer is responsible for contributing. Social Security constituted about 35% of the mandatory portion of the Federal budget or ~$739 Billion[19] in 2009.

---

18   http://en.wikipedia.org/wiki/Social_Security_(United_States)

19   http://www.usgovernmentspending.com/year2009_0.html

Social Security has become the government's de facto retirement fund, even though it was originally meant to help provide a wage for those Americans who had outlived all of their savings. It now finances the retirement for millions of Americans by guaranteeing a monthly wage after one's working years have completed. The Social Security Administration (SSA) pays current retirees from the contributions of all current workers in the FICA program. The system will have enough funding to cover all retirees as long as there are enough workers contributing. At the end of WWII in 1945, there were 42 workers to every retiree[20]. Today, that ratio approximates only 3 workers to every retiree and is expected to continue dwindling. At this pace, the fund will soon experience greater withdrawals than contributions, with some dire estimates projecting that date to be within the next decade, and insolvency of the entire system occurring within 15-20 years after that.

Regardless of whether the system will become insolvent, two facts are undeniable: first, the system is in drastic need of repair because it is built on a flawed approach that assumes there will always be plenty of workers for every retiree. Today, workers can begin drawing funds as early as 62 unless they have qualified medical disabilities allowing them to draw funds earlier, with full retirement age currently set at 65 – 67 depending on what year you were born; secondly, **do not make the mistake of allowing social security to be the financial basis for your retirement nest egg!** It just might not be there when it becomes your turn to collect. In addition, the relatively small amount

---

20   http://www.heritage.org/Press/Commentary/ed080905b.cfm

collected as monthly income upon retirement relative to the total amount contributed over an entire career does not give one the feeling that it was worth the effort. If you fail to financially plan for your future, and wind up in the position where social security is your major income source, chances are your standard of living will be diminished.

Medicare, like Social Security is a government program designed originally as a way for social security beneficiaries to obtain health insurance. It was one of the key pieces of legislation that Lyndon Johnson signed as part of his *Great Society* in 1965 and part of his overall *War on Poverty*. Like Social Security, it is a government entitlement program and is part of the non-discretionary (mandatory) spending umbrella. Another similarity to OASDI is that this social insurance program is funded through payroll taxes on all working American's salaries and is the second component to FICA. The current deduction from one's paycheck is 1.45% matched by an equivalent contribution by the employer.

In 2009, Medicare and related payments comprised 36% of the non-discretionary portion of the Federal budget. Combined with Social Security these two government programs spent ~$1.4 Trillion. Again, this is a staggering amount and like Social Security, Medicare is a program that is experiencing increasing withdrawals from retirees compared to a decreasing rate of growth in new contributions as the ratio of workers to retirees continues to decrease.

Earlier we discussed how budget deficits and trade deficits can negatively impact the value of the USD. This also adds to overall economic weakness because it can cheapen the value of your assets and make many imported goods that much more expensive, which is another manifestation of inflation. Given that every year, the Federal Government needs to raise > $1 Trillion just to meet the needs of Social Security and Medicare recipients (this figure will grow annually), massive deficits can be expected to be a part of our economy for years to come. Be aware that certain politicians will use this as an excuse to continue raising taxes on Americans. Remember that in the long run, tax increases will likely result in economic slowdowns (since it is capital no longer available in the private sector), and rising unemployment rates. In fact, over the last 50-60 years, it can be argued that the greatest increases in Federal tax revenue have occurred in periods following income and capital gains tax rate decreases, since they have spurred an economic revival and overall capital expansion. **The problem then seems to lie in government's inability to reduce their level of spending to match overall tax collections**[21].

DISCRETIONARY SPENDING

Discretionary spending covers fiscal spending on areas where no guaranteed benefits have been promised to beneficiaries. Discretionary spending made up roughly 40% of the entire Federal budget of $3.5 Trillion in 2009 (~$1.4 Trillion) and is comprised of two major categories: *Defense – Discretionary* and *Non-Defense Discretionary*. The largest component of spending that is not mandatory is directed at the Defense Department (DoD). Spending in this area

---

21   http://www.heritage.org/Research/Taxes/wm182.cfm

has risen sharply since 9/11/01 as the US financed the cost of two wars, Iraq and Afghanistan. In 2009, "Defense – Discretionary" spending approached $800 Billion. While the amount of spending on the military is and should be debated constantly in Congress and throughout our society, we should always remember that the number one duty of the US Government is to provide for the national security of its citizens.

Non-Defense discretionary spending covers all the remaining Government agencies we have omitted thus far. This would include the Departments of Education, Health and Human Services, Interior, Justice, Commerce, Transportation, the Environmental Protection Agency, NASA, etc... Total spending in these areas is less than $600 Billion. It is important to note that when debates on wasteful Government spending take place, non-defense discretionary spending is the only area targeted for spending slow-downs and/or reduction. This area only constitutes ~17% of total Government spending, since mandatory spending on entitlements, interest on the debt and a large portion of the military budget are areas in which the government is obligated to spend.

The rest of this book is geared towards providing guidance on keeping one's fiscal household in order and to live at or below your means. Translation: spend less than your take home pay. It is unfortunate that Americans have as an example a Government fraught with waste, fraud and abuse, where poor fiscal decisions put us all at a disadvantage through higher inflationary pressures, a cheapening currency and an enormous national debt with which our children and grandchildren will be saddled.

Summary / Tips to Remember
- Fiscal policy details how the government generates revenue (taxes) and spends money (expenditures) on non-discretionary (entitlements) and discretionary (defense/other) items
- Monetary policy's key objective is to control the nation's money supply with the goal of achieving sustainable economic growth, maximum employment and low inflation
- The Yield Curve reflects the relationship between interest rates and time to maturity. It can illustrate whether we are in a normal economic environment or headed for recessionary conditions.
- Inflation is the expansion of the money supply manifested by increases in general price levels; the Consumer and Producer Price Indices are key metrics that track inflation in the US economy.
- Budget deficits result from expenditures exceeding revenue on an annual basis; the National Debt is the accumulation of all annual budget deficits

(B) BUDGETING

SETTING GOALS

So much is made of setting goals but why are they important? Are they over-rated? Does one risk over-emphasizing certain desires in life at the expense of other areas that may be just as important? Possibly, but if you are not driving towards something, you will most likely achieve nothing!! Goals are the key to focusing one's energies. Once an individual realizes what it is he wants to accomplish in life, hard work is the engine that will allow that person to reach the milestones he has set. For the average individual who wishes to lead a balanced life, financial goals will likely include but not be limited to the elimination of debt, providing for one's family, and building a retirement nest egg. Goals are objectives which should be consistently monitored, measured, and fine-tuned. It is very easy to come up with blockbuster ideas only to see them go by the wayside because the individual lacks a **plan** and the persistence to continue working hard to accomplish those hopes and dreams.

Eliminating debt is arguably the most difficult financial objective to realize. It requires significant self-control, and if the household income stream is not very large, can be most difficult to accomplish. Credit card abuse is the easiest way to fall into the debt trap. Credit card companies begin the financial seduction early in a person's life. It often seems easier to obtain a credit card when a student is still in college than it is when they are out in the work force. Yet it is these individuals who are the most susceptible to incurring debt. Since most credit cards only require the buyer to pay a monthly minimum (approximately 2% of the total balance), it can take many years to pay off using this method. And this *assumes* that the debtor does not increase the total amount owed, which is highly unlikely, since spending habits will probably not have changed for the better.

To understand the impact of this cost, let's look at a real-life example: a person with a $1,000 balance paying a minimum 2% required payment with a 14 annual percentage rate (APR) would need to make payments over approximately 156 months before the balance would be paid off. **Not only does this constitute a full thirteen years of your life but it would equate to $935 worth of interest charges, almost as much as the original balance of the card**[22]. Although the time required to pay the balance on a credit card may not be foremost in the average person's mind, the fact is that significant amounts of money owed to credit card companies are in the form of interest and not just re-payment of the principal. **In essence, it is a huge waste of money, brought about by a fundamental lack of understanding of finances.**

---

22   http://www.womentodaymagazine.com/money/minimum_ payment.html

Returning to our conversation on goals, many individuals often have periodic spurts of inspiration in which the "light bulb" goes off and they determine what their hopes and dreams are, and become very excited about bringing them to fruition. In order to realize one's goals, which can take many years to accomplish, one needs to have a constant focus on what the end game is and be steadfast in reaching that goal. This is best accomplished through a detailed, realistic plan.

DEVELOPING A PLAN

A common adage states that "the difference between a goal and a dream is a plan." This is what separates daydreamers from the doers in life. From a financial perspective, there is a fabulous tool that is simple to construct yet incredibly difficult for many to follow. It is a *budget* or personal income statement. It is a monthly tabulation of the household income sources (the money you earn), less the total monthly expenses (the money you spend), to arrive at a net gain or net loss position for that period of time. It is one of the most critical ingredients of a personal financial plan because it allows an individual to prioritize when certain purchases should be made as well as how different debts should be disposed of, and it begins the process of instilling fiscal discipline in the household.

Before preparing a detailed family budget, it is imperative that you understand that salary level does not translate into your take home pay. This means that your annual salary divided by twelve months is not the money you have available to pay the monthly bills. Before you consider this line of thinking to be elemental, ask yourself the following question: for every dollar in salary, how many cents on the dollar do you bring home to pay the bills? The answer may shock you. I will submit to you that given our current tax landscape in America, and if you are contributing to a retirement nest egg and protecting your loved ones through a medical plan contribution, you might be bringing home as little as 60 – 70 cents out of every dollar in salary. *Only then do you get to start paying all the bills!!* How can this possibly compute? Let's look at the following example and then analyze the results:

Smith Family	Salary	Occupation
Steve	$ 75,000	Sales Manager
Susan	$ 40,000	Speech Therapist (PT)

As you can see, Steve Smith is the primary breadwinner in our fictitious household. Susan works part time and is a full time home-maker, as is the case with many moms in America these days. Combined, their annual household salary is $115,000, or approximately $9,583 per month. But what can they count on to pay the bills? Please note the following schedule and then analyze the subsequent steps:

Steve	$ 2,885	Bi-weekly Gross Pay
401K Deduction	(288)	10% Tax Deferred - Voluntary
Medical Benefits	(150)	Medical Plan - Voluntary
Taxable Income	$ 2,446	

Susan	$ 1,538	Bi-weekly Gross Pay
401K Deduction	(123)	8% Tax Deferred - Voluntary
Taxable Income	$ 1,415	

Step 1: Take each spouse's annual salary and divide by 26 to arrive at a bi-weekly gross salary, since most individuals are paid every other week

Step 2: Subtract the **voluntary deductions** from the bi-weekly gross annual salary to arrive at "taxable income"; voluntary deductions comprise two key categories: tax deferred savings plans (i.e.401Ks, 403Bs, IRAs), whose purpose is primarily directed at helping you fund your retirement nest egg without incurring taxes on those contributions. In addition, contributions to fund one's medical plans have historically been exempt from payroll withholding taxes as well. Notice that with medical plan contributions, only one spouse is expected to pay for these benefits, since it is usually cheaper and more efficient for one spouse to provide medical coverage for the entire household.

I cannot over-emphasize the importance of contributing to a tax deferred savings plan as well as a medical plan. The former allows you to build a substantial nest egg, without tax consequences until retirement, *providing the contributor with 30-40 years of wealth building opportunities that take advantage of interest rate compounding (more on this in the Investing chapter)*. Likewise, going without at least some inexpensive form of medical coverage would be irresponsible, especially if you have children. God forbid, if some catastrophic event occurs, you do not want to be saddled with staggering medical bills for a good portion of your lifetime.

At this point, you have arrived at taxable income. This is the income level which will be subject to statutory deductions – those mandatory withholding taxes used to fund the federal government, your respective state government, as well as Social Security and Medicare.

Steve	$	2,446	Taxable Income
Federal Withholding	$	(246)	28% Bracket - Statutory
State Withholding	$	(179)	MD State & County - Statutory
FICA - Social Security	$	(152)	6.2% of T/I - Statutory
FICA - Medicare	$	(35)	1.45% of T/I - Statutory
Take Home Pay	$	1,835	

Susan	$	1,415	Taxable Income
Federal Withholding	$	(91)	28% Bracket - Statutory
State Withholding	$	(97)	MD State & County - Statutory
FICA - Social Security	$	(88)	6.2% of T/I - Statutory
FICA - Medicare	$	(21)	1.45% of T/I - Statutory
Take Home Pay	$	1,119	

Step 3: Once you arrive at the bi-weekly **taxable income** total, your paycheck will reflect the subtraction of all statutory deductions to arrive at **net take home pay**[23]. Notice that the statutory withholding deductions are broken down into two categories: Income tax (Federal & State); and FICA payroll tax (Federal Insurance contributions Act). The former is calculated based on how much the household earns in income, and the latter is arrived at using predetermined tax rates assessed on your taxable income. As you can see, once the retirement and medical plan contributions are made, and once the various withholding taxes are applied, the combined take home pay for the household is approximately 67% of gross pay. This is the figure that households should base all spending decisions on, and NOT their respective salaries.

---

23   http://www.payroll-taxes.com/

Spouse	Gross Pay	Net Pay	%
Steve	2,885	$ 1,835	63.6%
Susan	1,538	$ 1,119	72.8%
Household	$ 4,423	$ 2,954	66.8%

Now that we have identified what each spouse contributes in take home pay, the Smith's can develop their monthly budget. Remember that the payments we have outlined above represent bi-weekly amounts, since that is how most working Americans are paid. To develop a monthly budget or personal income statement, which is what I would recommend as a tracking mechanism, simply convert the take home pay amounts by multiplying by 26 (total pay periods in a year) and dividing by 12 (total months), as illustrated in the Smith budget below:

Smith Monthly Budget		
Steve Take Home Pay	$ 3,975	
Susan Take Home Pay	$ 2,425	
Total Household Income	$ 6,400	
Mortgage	$ 1,507	
Car Payment	$ 321	
Car Insurance	$ 163	
Day Care	$ 575	2 Days / week
Credit Cards (minimum)	$ 130	
Visa		80
MasterCard		50
Food	$ 900	
Student Loans	$ 173	
Gasoline	$ 200	
Cable / Internet / Phones	$ 175	
Gym Membership (Family)	$ 125	
Gas / Electric	$ 260	
Car / Home Maintenance	$ 100	Reserve Fund
Water	$ 35	
Security	$ 40	
Miscellaneous	$ 150	Cleaners / Church, other
Total Monthly Bills	$ 4,855	
Disposable Income	$ 1,545	

In this example, the family's disposable income is $1,545 per month. This is money that can be used for entertainment, savings for unanticipated expenses, future goals such as funding a child's college education or a wedding, etc. In addition, for households that do not own their primary residence, disposable income is what should be used to fund down-payments, as well as closing cost obligations on newly purchased homes.

This handbook is primarily aimed at young Americans, aged 18-24 because it is at this point where individuals in all likelihood have not yet developed poor spending habits, and where long term wealth building can begin without significant debt burdens to overcome. That being said, the previous budget illustrates a typical homeowner's monthly budget; i.e., someone at least in their late 20's or early 30's if not older. Most individuals in their early 20's will not own their homes. They will likely be living at home with their parents, living in some college dormitory or renting an apartment or house with friends. These individuals will have little to no income to speak of, because they will either not be working or they will be earning relatively little income since their lack of work experience and education will not allow most of them to command salary levels commensurate with running a household. This situation is expected. It is not a reason to panic.

It is assumed that if someone in their early 20's prepares a budget, there is a strong likelihood that spending will be greater than income generated, resulting in a monthly disposable loss situation. In addition, they may be incurring debt as a result of student loan borrowing, purchasing a car to be able to go to work if they have a job, and by using credit cards to purchase food and/or other necessities.

The key for young people in this situation is to limit their spending to the maximum extent possible. It does not make sense to purchase an expensive car which will be accompanied by hefty car payments if they are not generating sufficient income with which to pay the car. It does not make sense to attend expensive graduate schools if they plan on obtaining employment that is not expected to provide significant earning opportunities. For instance, attending an Ivy League Law School in order to take a Public Defender's job in a small town may have significant qualitative merits, but from a financial perspective, it will result in massive student loan debt being incurred, without the long term ability to pay off that debt. Given the effects of compounding interest, it becomes very difficult to pay off that debt and can quickly lead to financial ruin.

Whether a student graduating from college or a parent running a household, a budget serves as a tool which can instantly shed light on areas of personal finance that need improvement, whether from an income generating standpoint or an expense reduction perspective. There are many ways to improve your monthly income to expense ratio. On the income side, you can generate more income by doing the following:

- Obtain a promotion or raise in your current position
- Find a new job with your current company or a different company using your present skills
- Return to school to obtain a degree in a field that is in greater financial demand
- Obtain a part-time job in addition to your full-time job to supplement your income stream

From a cost control perspective, there are less obvious, but just as many, opportunities to improve your disposable income at the end of each month:

- Consolidate your credit cards to one low monthly payment and destroy the other cards, which will save you considerable interest expense in the long run.
- If you are a handyman, you can cut large labor costs by performing home maintenance activities yourself such as painting, roofing, electrical work, etc.
- Perform routine preventive maintenance on your automobile, which will reduce the cost of more expensive repairs in the long run.
- Drive safely to ensure you obtain the lowest, most competitive auto insurance rates. Young people need to realize that auto insurance, similar to life insurance, is the purchase of protection against automobile accidents resulting in personal injury, car damage, and a whole host of additional expenses. Contrary to what some young people might think, insurance is not a deposit they will be reimbursed for at a later time, but a lifetime asset protection tool.

- Pay your monthly bills on time. This will guarantee that you will achieve the best credit rating possible and allow you to obtain the best mortgage and credit card rates at such time as you buy a home or use a credit card.
- "Clip coupons" out of your local newspaper to reduce your grocery bills. What may seem a boring endeavor, can reduce your monthly expenses by hundreds of dollars over the course of a year.

I would pose a challenge to you: consider every expense item in your budget a **variable expense**, meaning that you have the ability to reduce that cost through creative thinking. There is always a way to cut costs.

As you can see, there are many ways you can improve your financial position. It requires hard work, creativity, dedication, and the willingness to perform new money-saving tasks. As far as adding additional income, many people are often unwilling to change employment because they become comfortable with the status quo. At the end of the day, you have to enjoy what you do for a living or else it can be a miserable existence. If you have a job you enjoy, keep it. However, do not be unwilling to take on a new challenge that can bring long-term satisfaction as well as improve your financial position. From a cost control standpoint, the high cost of labor in the United States has forced many individuals to learn new skills in order to avoid being subjected to high costs. As mentioned in the examples I cite, home maintenance costs over time can put a significant dent in one's monthly budget. It would behoove all of us to learn new skills which will go a long way toward improving the bottom line.

Before proceeding to the chapter covering debt elimination, I would like to focus on one area of personal finance that young people will face immediately upon leaving their parents' household. They will eventually be confronted with the responsibility of maintaining a bank account and balancing a checkbook or an on-line billing account. What seems to be an easy task can present some confusion for young people because they sometimes misunderstand how much money they truly have to spend.

Many times, people will withdraw funds from a bank account and through a receipt, obtain an immediate view of how much money remains in the account. If checks have been recently written against the account, they may be in the process of being posted against the individual's account (outstanding checks) and the sum total of those recently written checks may not be reflected in the ATM receipt the individual is holding. The end result may be that this person writes additional checks against the account and ends up "bouncing" the checks, meaning that not enough funds are in the account to cover the amount of the check. Not only does this usually result in a fine against the individual, but repeated check bouncing episodes can result in a bad credit record, which may impact the individual down the line through higher interest rates on credit cards and the inability to qualify for a home mortgage. This is one area where a little attention to detail can go a long way toward mitigating future heartache for individuals.

Two ways to avoid this are to reconcile your checkbook on a monthly basis. This is done by performing the following calculation:

Beginning account balance for the period in question

(+) **deposits** into the account during the period (includes payroll deposits / checks received, etc…)

(+) **deposits-in-transit** (deposits coming into the account that have not yet materialized)

(-) all **expenses** during the period (ATM withdrawals / debit transactions / checks, etc…)

(-) **outstanding checks** (checks you have written, which have not been posted to your account yet)

Equals ending account balance

An additional way to ensure your account correctly reflects all transactions is to maintain a daily log of **all** expenses and deposits affecting your account (I do this by maintaining a spreadsheet with all debits and credits to the account. Either method will ensure that you avoid any account overdrafts for which you will be penalized and see your credit report affected.

Summary / Tips to Remember
- Maximizing household net worth should be the over-arching financial objective for every household. It provides a long term focus critical to proper decision-making.

- Budgets are *planning tools.* They allow households to determine whether they are living within their means as well as to identify cost reduction opportunities to maximize disposable income.
- Gross salary does **NOT** = take home pay. After the typical deductions households will typically bring home 65c to 75c on the $; the net pay is the money available for paying monthly bills.
- Voluntary deductions fund a household's retirement nest egg on a tax deferred basis and pay for medical expenses
- Statutory deductions are mandated by law and help fill the government's income tax and payroll tax coffers
- Disposable income should be used to fund "rainy day" accounts, down-payments, and large planned expenses (i.e. weddings, vacations) that might be excluded from the monthly budget.

(E) ELIMINATING DEBT

For millions of people, debt is the 800-pound gorilla that prevents them from achieving financial freedom and forces them to work well into their golden years. The key to long term financial success for most people is determined not by how much you make in income, but rather how much you keep after all the bills are paid. As I mentioned in the opening section, calculate the sum total of all your assets (bank accounts, savings accounts, investments, properties, etc.), subtract all your liabilities (loan balances, mortgage debt, credit card debts, etc.), and the remainder is your net worth—or net loss if your liabilities exceed your assets. I do not consider "monthly bills" to be debt. Debt is a liability that carries a balance that is not paid in the current period. Bills are in essence the cost of daily living.

Certain individuals, primarily entrepreneurs, are perfectly comfortable with a **manageable** debt level because they feel they can borrow funds from banks or other financial institutions and turn those funds into greater wealth than they would be able to generate without that source of funding. That's fine but it entails undertaking greater amounts of risk than many people are comfortable in assuming. I contend most Americans are more interested in leading a debt-free existence. Following are some household debt statistics for average Americans:

- The average American household in 2010 has thirteen total credit obligations on record at a credit bureau.[24] Of this total as many as nine will likely be credit card obligations. This includes consumer credit cards (i.e. VISA, MasterCard), retail store credit cards (i.e. Nordstrom, Macys), debit cards, etc. My question is: *what are you thinking?* I would argue that a household needs no more than one credit card and / or debit card (which is the same as a cash card). A key reason that Americans reach debt positions which are unmanageable is that they lose control of their liabilities.

- In early 2010, the average household consumer credit card balance was about $7,400.[25] This balance has risen by 2.5x, up from approximately $3,000 per household in 1990. To be fair, this total is calculated by adding up all consumer credit card debt and dividing it by the total number of households nationwide. This can lead to some misleading assumptions that the typical household maintains an average credit card balance of $7,400. Most people are more frugal than that, but the fact remains that as a nation we continue to increase our total consumer debt balance, now totaling more than $874 billion dollars!!!

---

24   http://www.creditcards.com/statistics/credit-card-industry-facts-and-personal-debt-statistics.php

25   http://www.indexcreditcards.com/creditcarddebt/

o It should be noted that average credit card balance per household has been higher in recent memory, peaking at ~$9,000 within the last 5 years. The sub-prime mortgage crisis and ensuing recession caused a lot of households to take some of their investment losses, cash them out and pay down high credit card balances.

Undoubtedly, the credit card companies' marketing campaigns, which involve saturating college campuses by offering students free credit, are a large contributor to this growth in consumer debt. Today, college undergraduate students have approximately 3 credit cards[26] on average, and ½ of undergraduates have more than 4 credit cards with an average credit card balance of more than $3,100[27]. Before proceeding with the reasons that credit card debt snowballs, it is important to understand what a credit card is. From the buyer's standpoint, using a credit card is nothing more than a loan request to the vendor in question with almost instantaneous approval. At the time a purchase is made with a credit card, the consumer has paid for NOTHING! The individual has only made a promise that payment will be made at a later date, usually within thirty days. Many of us have the misconception that the purchased product has already been paid. NOTHING COULD BE FURTHER FROM THE TRUTH.

As a society, there are many policies in place by creditors which actually end up encouraging people to charge

---

26   http://www.ucms.com/college-credit-card-statistics.htm

27   http://www.creditcards.com/statistics/credit-card-industry-facts-and-personal-debt-statistics.php

more on their cards. People have the somewhat mistaken assumption that by charging larger sums on their credit cards, they are actually establishing good credit which will eventually enable them to qualify for favorable mortgage rates, auto loan rates, etc... While this is somewhat true, there is little incentive to curtail spending, since most credit card companies only require individuals to pay a minimum, usually a pre-set balance or approximately 2 percent of their loan balance. The actual payment terms are described in the fine print on your credit agreement. Why would credit card companies do this? The answer is simple. Credit companies make significant amounts of money on interest earned. If everyone paid the full amount each month, credit card companies would make much less money and would have to rely much more on certain fees and surcharges they impose.

Evidently, there are competing objectives for consumers and credit card companies. Another policy which companies employ, resulting in debt accumulation, is to increase credit card limits for consumers. Often times, if an individual approaches the pre-set credit limit, additional credit may be granted by making a quick phone call. If that credit limit is reached, the company holding the charge card may disallow any additional spending or "max out" the credit card. Many of these consumers, faced with a situation in which they cannot borrow on that card anymore, find ways to obtain a new credit card and begin the process anew, further exacerbating the situation.

From a marketing standpoint, credit card companies use another enticing strategy to attract customers. Gold and platinum cards offer consumers the opportunity to win free trips, hotel stays, mileage awards, and other wonderful gifts. What consumer would not be attracted to these promotions? The consumer needs to use good judgment and should be aware of all the ancillary costs that come with some of these cards. To reiterate, there is once again no need to have more than one credit card for all your purchases. Being disciplined prevents you from amassing too much credit by limiting your total exposure to one card. Second, be aware that some of these gold or platinum cards come with very high annual fees and potentially high interest rates. The annual fees are one-time expenses the credit card company charges the consumer for the privilege of using their card and taking advantage of the promotions they offer.

Also, beware of department store credit cards. The most common strategy for credit card companies is to offer consumers a discount on their first purchase as long as they sign up for the credit card. After that first purchase is made, the consumer winds up paying very high interest rates for any balances at the end of a particular month, often exceeding those of the major credit card companies.

Finally, there is a popular practice in the retail industry, which is to sell consumers big-ticket items with "no money down" and "no interest expenses" for a specific period of time. The retailers further entice the consumer with guarantees that their monthly payments for the item in question will be for low amounts. Before you proceed, please keep in mind that, once again, NOTHING has been paid for; although you may be deferring monthly bills, you have assumed an additional liability or debt balance which reduces your household net worth. I would caution the individual to read the fine print and understand the interest rates she is being subjected to and the total number of payments she is agreeing to make. Chances are it will take a protracted period of time to complete the purchase, during which time the individual may sign up for several more of these "great deals."

What many individuals seem to forget is that the "good" credit they are trying to establish will only occur if they make payments on time and spend within their means. Purchasing goods using new credit cards under "no money down" initial payment terms still raises the level of household debt. By raising household debt, consumers are actually placing themselves in a position where they are in danger of maxing out their credit cards, which will result in mortgage companies or auto financing companies charging higher rates of interest to the consumer since they are now perceived to be a greater credit risk.

To put this issue into perspective, let's assume the average American household owes in the neighborhood of $9,000 in credit card bills. If we apply a standard annual percentage rate (APR) of 13 percent (for a person with good credit) and assume the debtor pays a monthly minimum of $150, it will take ninety-seven months, or just over eight years, to pay the total bill.[28] This results in a total payment of $14,550 to the credit card company **due to $5,550 in interest charges**. More important, this scenario assumes that your overall balance will not rise over time. This is highly unlikely, since it would require a significant change

28   http://www.bankrate.com/calculators/credit-cards/credit-card-payoff-calculator.aspx

in spending behavior. Empirical evidence has shown that many people who are able to bring down their debt balance by a significant amount often go back into similar levels of debt as they no longer view the problem as serious. The interest charges are a complete waste of money and the result of bad budgeting and a lack of understanding of basic fundamentals of finance. **To get out of debt you must change your spending habits!!**

Why, then, do so many Americans allow themselves to be in such a perilous financial situation? There are a whole host of reasons, but the following answers come to mind:

- **"Keeping up with the Joneses"**: It may be human nature but in our culture there is an insidious penchant to accumulate material possessions in order to feel that you somehow belong to a particular social stratum. Individuals end up making poor investment decisions and spending more than they earn in order to generate some sort of self-satisfaction. For adults, this trait was never more evident than the late 1990s stock market boom where individuals would purchase common stock in any internet or technology firm they could find, in order to boast about their portfolios at the next cocktail party. In this decade, this attitude was reflected in the housing bubble that took place between 2002 and 2006 where home values soared at unprecedented growth rates marked by an atmosphere of "panic" buying, where individuals purchased primary residences and second homes for prices far in excess of their true worth, because "they had to have it". For young people, the types of purchases differ but the behavior is the same. Teenagers and college-aged Americans routinely buy fashionable and trendy items, such as clothes, "I-Pods", "I-Phones", "Droids", cars and jewelry, to be able to make a statement to peers that they "belong" and fit into a particular group. No one wants to feel like an outcast, and unfortunately, this often contributes to poor financial decisions.

- **Impatience:** As a nation, we have never been more affluent than we are today. Median household income in 2009 was \$49,777.[29] In 1980 this same figure was \$17,710. If you use an average annual inflation rate of 2.6 percent (as measured by the Consumer Price Index from 1980 – 2010)[30] over that time span, you would still realize a 29% percent growth in household income, net of inflation. Yet, even as our real income has grown as a society, we have accumulated greater personal debt than at any time during our lives. It is my contention that people today do not share the thrifty values of past generations. We have this compulsion to buy anything we want, when we want it, without any apparent consideration for having the where-withal to pay for the items in question and with little regard to saving for retirement. It took our parents decades to acquire a household worth of

---

29   http://www.census.gov/newsroom/releases/archives/income_
wealth/cb10-144.html

30   http://inflationdata.com/inflation/Consumer_Price_Index/
HistoricalCPI.aspx?rsCPI_currentPage=2

furnishings because they were sacrificing their own desires to raise their families and to put funds away for a rainy day, as well as retirement. In fact, statistics show that a typical pre-retiree household (age 55 and up) only has approximately $60,000 in savings[31], and as many as 96 percent of Americans will retire financially dependent on the government[32] (meaning they will rely, in some measure, on Social Security), and that the average U.S. household in 2005 had a total spending balance greater than the total income generated for the first time ever, compared to a 11.1 percent savings rate in 1985.[33] This is an astounding figure and shows just how far we have come in our national spending binge.

- **Spending Binges**: Certain individuals are predisposed to spending money as long as they have access to it. Some of the best examples are uncontrollable shoppers, those who buy clothing and other items without regard as to whether they need the products or not. Instilling fiscal discipline is essential for those pre-disposed to go on spending binges. One way to prevent this from happening is to self impose a 24 **hour spending moratorium**: that is, if the price of a desired item exceeds a certain dollar amount, don't buy it right away. Wait at least a day in which you will be able to determine if you have a real need for this item, or if its purchase will merely placate a passing whim.

31   http://www.zero2rich.com/average-retirement-savings.html
32   http://www.progressiverelief.com/consumer-debt-statistics.html
33   http://www.bankrate.com/brm/news/sav/20060308a1.asp

Now that we understand some of the reasons why Americans accumulate such a large debt position, we need to explore how to get out of the hole. The first rule should be to never enter into consumer debt (credit card / personal debt) in the first place, but if that occurs, the following principles employed with the proper discipline will assist you in extricating yourself from this negative cash flow position:

- **Income > Costs: Costs should not exceed income on a consistent basis!**
  There may be occasions where one might fall into this precarious financial position: a layoff, a large, one-time unbudgeted payment, a medical incident, etc… However, income that is consistently less than expenses will spell financial disaster in the long term. If you remember nothing else, remember that IT'S NOT WHAT YOU MAKE, IT'S WHAT YOU KEEP! There are numerous examples of people who earn millions of dollars a year, yet file for bankruptcy or come close to filing due to out of control spending habits (think Elton John).
  For those who are binge spenders, there are two suggestions which can truly rein in uncontrollable spending. First, prepare a detailed budget which not only lists all income and regular monthly expenses, but should also define how much discretionary spending you are able to undertake. Once you have isolated a specific amount of "fun" spending you can afford, stick to that figure and always try to spend less than that amount. Finally, even if you can afford an expense, ask yourself the question, "Do I need this item?"

- **Live Within (or Preferably Below) Your Means**
  We need to accept the fact that our current income
  levels afford a certain standard of living. If you are
  not happy with your present circumstances, then you
  have the freedom to go back to school and obtain
  a higher level of education or learn a specific trade,
  enabling you to make more money and afford a
  higher standard of living. However, until the income
  level rises, it is imperative that spending remains in
  line with income. Learn to live at least within your
  means, but preferably below your means. By maximizing your disposable income today, you will be able
  to have additional savings for retirement, and greater
  overall flexibility in your finances. As an example, living below one's means will allow a parent to add to a
  child's college fund, such as a 529 Plan or other types
  of savings accounts specifically targeted at educational
  expenses. Living below one's means allows a young
  couple to maintain an emergency fund, available for
  unanticipated household expenses such as a new roof
  for the house. The appropriate level of money in an
  emergency fund is subject to different interpretation
  but a rule of thumb is to have at least six months of
  salary available in cash, because that is the average
  time it takes to replace one's employment at similar
  salary levels, should one or both parents have the mis-
  fortune of losing their employment.
- **Reduce Total Creditors: Less creditors = more
  manageable expenses**
  One way of controlling credit card burdens is to
  consolidate credit cards at one low, fixed rate. This

can be done via home equity loans (if you own a
home) and other loan consolidation programs. In
addition, home equity loans (to be discussed in
more detail later) include the added feature of tax
deductibility on a portion of the payment.

- **Accelerate Debt Payments**
  By maintaining discipline and applying a few
  tricks of the trade, you can truly accelerate the rate
  at which you can eliminate all of your outstanding
  debt. The following example, taken from the budget shown in the previous chapter and reflected in
  Step 1, illustrates the number of months it will
  take to pay off the current debt balances for the
  Smith household under normal circumstances:

Debt Acceleration Example - Step 1

Obligation	Balance Due	Rate	Monthly Payment	Payoff Months	Total Interest Owed
Car Payment	$ 17,500	4%	$ 321	60	$ 1,837
Student Loans	15,000	7%	173	120	5,778
Visa	4,000	18%	80	92	3,360
MasterCard	2,500	21%	50	116	3,300
Total Debt	$ 39,000		$ 624	120	$ 14,275

As you can see, the non-mortgage debt totals
$39,000. The total monthly payments (within the
family budget) directed towards these obligations is
$624. The monthly payments for the car and student
loans are calculated based on the present value (more

on this in the Home Ownership chapter) of the money borrowed, which incorporates the respective interest rates and the maturity life of each loan. Another way of stating this is "what monthly payment is required to pay the loan balance in full assuming a particular interest rate and total number of loan payments"? The credit card payments are based on 2% minimums (a typical credit card repayment structure) of the outstanding debt balances. Therefore, it will take the Smith family 120 months or 10 years to pay off the $39,000 loan balances + more than $14,000 in corresponding interest costs assuming **no additional debt** is incurred during this time.

What if the Smith's decided to accelerate those loan payments? How would they accomplish this objective and maintain fidelity towards the rest of the obligations in their budget? Recall from the family's budget in the previous chapter that the Smith's generated a disposable income of **$1,545** each month after the bills were paid. Assume that a lot of that disposable income goes towards additional savings, entertainment, vacation funds, etc... Let's further assume that they are able to contribute an additional $250 per month toward eliminating these debts. How would we distribute the additional $250? If you understand compounding interest and how it works for you as well as against you, those additional monies should be directed at the obligations carrying the highest annual interest rate, regardless of how large or how small their respective debt balances are. That is because consumer debt which carries exorbitant annual interest rates, has the greatest ability to snowball against you. Step 2 illustrates how this would work.

Debt Acceleration Example - Step 2

Obligation	Balance Due	Rate	Monthly Payment	Payoff in Months	Total Interest
Car Payment	$ 17,500	4%	$ 321	60	$ 1,837
Student Loans	15,000	7%	173	120	5,778
Visa	4,000	18%	80	92	3,360
MasterCard + Add'l	2,500	21%	300	10	500
Total Debt	$ 39,000		$ 874	120	$ 11,475

Comparing Step 2 to Step 1 shows that by adding an extra $250 to the original monthly payment total of $624, allows the Smith's to pay the MasterCard balance in 10 months; a full 106 months earlier than they would have had they just paid the minimum amount required. In addition, the Smith's will only incur $500 of interest costs by accelerating their payments – *a savings of $2,800 from the original obligation!!* Total debt payoff is still scheduled to occur over 120 months because that is the length of time currently required to pay off the student loans, but that too will be addressed.

Once the MasterCard debt is paid in full, the idea would be to *continue paying a total of $874* a month towards the remaining debt balances to accelerate the elimination of the debt. This would result in a $380 monthly payment going forward to satisfy the

Visa payment, which carries the next highest annual interest rate. Step 3 illustrates how this would occur.

Debt Acceleration Example - Step 3					
Obligation	Balance Due	Rate	Monthly Payment	Payoff in Months	Total Interest
Car Payment	$ 14,820	4%	$ 321	50	$ 1,837
Student Loans	14,110	7%	173	110	5,778
Visa + Additional	3,804	18%	380	11	980
MasterCard	-				500
Total Debt	$ 32,734		$ 874	110	$ 9,095

As you can see, the total remaining debt balance after the MasterCard is paid off will be reduced to < $33,000. The total number of months until payoff reflects a reduction for the car payment and student loan which assumes that those payments have been continuing as normal over the 10 months it took to pay off the MasterCard. Given the additional $380 now allocated to pay off the Visa, it will only take an additional 11 months to pay off the remaining balance of $3,804, rather than the original 92 months it was going to take, a savings of 71 months and $2,360 in additional interest savings, since the Smith's will only incur a total of $980 in Visa interest costs.

Let's take stock of where we are: at this point, we are now only 21 months into the payoff process, and 2 of the 4 debt balances have been completely eliminated. The original timetable to eliminate this debt was 10 years, so tremendous progress has already been made. In addition, the 2 credit card payments resulted in a total of $1,380 of interest, a savings of $5,280 for the Smith's since they were scheduled to pay $6,660 in interest for these two obligations, had they continued making minimum payments!!

After these 21 months we will assume the Smith's are still gainfully employed and are able to continue paying $874 towards the remaining debt balances (car + student loans). Step 4 reflects how this will be accomplished:

Debt Acceleration Example - Step 4					
Obligation	Balance Due	Rate	Monthly Payment	Payoff in Months	Total Interest
Car Payment	$ 11,768	4%	$ 321	39	$ 1,837
Student Loans	13,070	7%	553	24	1,912
Visa	-				980
MasterCard	-				500
Total Debt	$ 24,838		$ 874	39	$ 5,229

In the same manner in which the prior two debt balances were targeted, the Smith's have decided to aggressively pay down the student loan debt since it carries the highest annual interest rate of the remaining two debt obligations. Using a loan repayment calculator, the Smith's determine that in another 24 months they can fully pay off the college debt. Rather than taking 10 years or 120 months to pay this off in the original example, they will be able to eliminate this entire debt balance in 45 months or a little less than 4 years. In addition, their total interest burden for this item will be $1,912. Had they taken the full 10 years to pay off this loan they would have paid $5,778. **They will end up saving $3,866 in interest costs**, just by living within their means and being extremely judicious in how they apply discretionary income.

We have one final step remaining and that is to address the remaining car loan balance. Step 5 will walk us through this:

Debt Acceleration Example - Step 5					
Obligation	Balance Due	Rate	Monthly Payment	Payoff in Months	Total Interest
Car Payment	$ 4,708	4%	$ 874	5.5	$ 1,779
Student Loans	-				1,912
Visa	-				980
MasterCard	-				500
Total Debt	$ 4,708		$ 874	5.5	$ 5,171

Remember that after Step 4 which addressed the student loan balance, the Smith's still had about 15 months remaining on their car loan, since they had been paying down that debt according to the original schedule which spread the car payments over 60 months. Using the same $874 that was set aside within their budgets to pay down these debt balances, they will be able to pay off the remaining amount on the loan in just over 5 months, rather than the 15 left on the loan. They will end up paying $1,779 in interest on the car loan rather than the $1,837 originally expected to be paid, resulting in a small savings of $58 in interest. Now that we have the full picture, let's review some of the highlights:

- All 4 debt balances totaling $39,000 have been eliminated
- It will take the Smith's 50 months to pay the entire non-mortgage debt, rather than the original 120 months. By using debt acceleration principles they will be able to pay the total off in 42% of the expected time – *a savings of 70 months or almost 6 years!!*
- The total interest paid on top of the $39,000 debt is $5,171, *saving $9,104* from the original expected total – just by living within / below their means

If we can save so much in interest and rid ourselves of debt in such a seemingly easy fashion, why don't more people do this? One mistake many individuals of all ages make is that once a particular debt obligation has been fulfilled, the monthly savings generated from no longer having to make that payment are often considered to be new money! That is, many people will consider this to be part of their disposable income and will spend this "extra" money on discretionary items. Some young people are wont to spend much of their disposable income on partying and frivolity. Others are fiscally responsible from day one. I can't begin to count how much money I wasted on trivial items during my

20's. While I am not expecting all young people to adopt a fiscally responsible behavior overnight, I do recommend you take stock of just how much money you might spend on partying, music, clothes, and other forms of entertainment.

Another reason that debt levels tend to rise again after an existing loan is paid in full is that new obligations come into play. I believe this is the key reason why individuals should attempt to live at or below their means if at all possible, since any new obligations may be mitigated through the use of emergency or other rainy day funds (remember that in the budget example I included a line item for home maintenance, which can double as a reserve fund). It is safe to assume, particularly for young people, that income streams or salaries will continue to grow incrementally until the age of fifty to fifty-five. As a result, proper planning will allow for additional disposable income to be created by having greater monthly income, without having to resort to spending the savings generated by the elimination of one debt obligation. As we have seen, the reapplication of these savings to remaining debt obligations can accelerate the elimination of all household debt.

By this point in your financial assessment, you will have achieved the following:

- Realized that your financial success will be measured in terms of how much net worth you have attained. This will necessitate that you maximize your level of personal assets while reducing / eliminating your total liabilities

- Set challenging but achievable goals you would like to accomplish; i.e. send children to college, buy a primary residence or second home, etc...
- Created a budget that ensures you are properly contributing to a tax deferred savings account, highlights all monthly obligations in order to cut costs where possible, and developed a cost tracking methodology to ensure you are sticking to your budget which can prove very difficult
- Identified a method to reduce / eliminate debt as quickly as possible

With respect to debt elimination, I recommend a proper order of debt reduction. Those debts or outstanding loans containing the highest interest rates should be disposed of first. Consumer debt or credit cards normally carry the highest interest rates and it is critical that individuals target these first. Automobile loan payments do not offer any tax deductibility features, so if the annual interest rates are comparable to the student loan rates, I would likely target the car payment next on the list of a payment acceleration plan. Finally, student loan interest should be next in line once the prior non-mortgage debts have been eliminated. In this case, there are some tax deductibility features and they are usually accompanied by relatively low interest rates. By following these simple steps, you will be in a position to start incrementing your asset base through the purchase of your first home.

CREDIT SCORING

The title of the book includes 6 steps I believe are crucial to achieving financial freedom:

- Budgeting
- Debt Elimination
- Home Ownership
- Investing
- Nursing / Long Term Care Insurance Costs
- Death Preparation (Estate Planning)

Although one can achieve wealth and maximize net worth in multiple ways, I believe it makes sense to follow these 6 steps in some logical order. First, you should assess your household financial situation by taking stock of whether the take home pay after all deductions is sufficient to afford your current standard of living. In addition, it is crucial that through your voluntary deductions that contributions to a tax friendly retirement plan are being made to the maximum extent possible. All of this can be accomplished by tracking faithfully to a budget. Second, address all outstanding debt and identify ways of minimizing or eliminating it altogether through debt consolidation and / or acceleration strategies. In taking these first two steps, you will mitigate your liabilities allowing for significant asset building to begin taking place. This will be largely accomplished through home ownership which we will see in the next chapter. How then, do we ensure that we can obtain the necessary financing to purchase a home at the best available rates? It is during the debt elimination phase that I strongly encourage a review of your credit score.

Most individuals do not have the available cash to purchase big ticket items such as a car, a residence, or an education. As such, most will need to borrow the money. The loan will then be accompanied by an annual interest rate that will correlate to the lending institution's perceived risk of issuing a loan to that person. FICO® scores are the credit scores most lenders use to determine your credit risk.[34] These scores are sourced by lending institutions accessing three main credit bureaus run by Experian, Equifax and Trans Union.[35] The term FICO® comes from Fair Isaac and Company, the firm that created the software that developed the scoring system.

The objective is to maximize your score, which typically ranges from 300 to 850. The higher the score, the less you will be considered a risk by lending institutions, because it indicates that you pay your bills on time, don't carry excess debt, and in all likelihood you have fewer debt obligations than those individuals with lower scores. Individuals with scores exceeding 700 are generally considered to be low risk candidates, allowing them to qualify for the best interest rates available in the marketplace for the loan in question. As the score begins to dip below 700, you begin to be perceived as a greater credit risk by lenders, providing them with the justification to increase the annual interest rate they will charge you for the financing you are hoping to obtain.

So how do you know what your FICO score is? By law, each citizen is allowed one free credit report annually. Many companies will provide this information, and they are

---

34   http://www.myfico.com/crediteducation/creditscores.aspx
35   Ibid

all accessible via the Internet. I strongly recommend that each year you access this information, because it provides one with the opportunity to determine whether creditors believe you pay your bills on time, to find out if there are any debt obligations that are still outstanding that you have long forgotten, and will also help you ensure that no one has stolen your identity. Identity theft is a massive problem in the United States. Each year, tens of thousands of Americans are victims of identity theft, resulting in potentially severe damage to one's credit rating, as criminals seek to purchase big ticket items using your name.

BANKRUPTCY

There are times that individuals wind up in such a financial predicament that there is no recourse but to declare personal bankruptcy. While this should be a last resort for anyone due to serious consequences on one's credit rating, lifestyle, etc.., we should acknowledge that the ability to declare bankruptcy serves as a protection for consumers and businesses from their creditors should the situation warrant it. Bankruptcies can occur for a variety of reasons.

From a household or personal level, often times, individuals lack spending discipline; that is, they spend money on objects they desire with little regard as to whether they can afford them. Over time, these poor spending habits result in the accumulation of significant amounts of consumer and / or personal debt which carries very high annual interest rates, due to the unsecured nature of the debt.[36] This type

---

36   http://www.ehow.com/about_5443981_types-unsecured-debt.
     html

of debt can easily mushroom if the consumer pays the creditor in minimum or small installments. Although no debt is technically good if your goal is to build wealth, consumer debt is the one with the greatest potential of spiraling out of control.

Living a lifestyle that is beyond one's means can also eventually lead to bankruptcy. Consider the individual who places a significant emphasis on reaching a high social stratum – "**Keeping up with the Jones'**". He is likely to purchase a late model, expensive automobile, buy a "pricey" home, own expensive clothes, and live a very high-cost lifestyle. Should this person lose his job as a result of a layoff or something completely out of his control, he would be in a very difficult position, unless he had sufficient savings available to tide him over until he was able to land a comparable job. Experts will tell you that it often takes 6-9 months to find such a position. Throw in a recession and this period could extend far beyond this time frame. Unless this person maintains a rainy day fund as part of his budget, he will likely go further into debt, exacerbating an already precarious situation.

One other not infrequent cause of personal bankruptcy filings is a large, unplanned medical cost. If you suffer an accident of some sort, or are stricken by a crippling disease that generates medical costs that far outweigh any medical insurance coverage you have, you may find yourself in a position where declaring personal bankruptcy is the only option to seek protection from creditors. Such a situation would likely result in your inability to work for a protracted period of time, making a difficult situation even worse by precluding any ability to generate income to pay the monthly bills.

These are not the only causes of personal bankruptcy; however, they are very common contributors and most of these can be avoided with proper planning and discipline. Budgeting properly, living within your means, accelerated targeting of existing debt balances are all at your disposal. It may require some hard decisions and self sacrifice from time to time, but depending on your commitment to achieving your household goals, you should be able to muster the fortitude to deal with most issues as they arise.

BANKRUPTCY OPTIONS

Definition: Inability to pay bills as they come due. Once you have reached this unfortunate position, and have made the decision to file bankruptcy and seek protection from your creditors (those you owe money to), it is incumbent upon you to choose the proper avenue in bankruptcy. The term bankruptcy does not necessarily mean you are penniless - quite the contrary; you have just reached a point where you cannot meet your short term obligations. In this book, we will explore two of the most common alternatives available to individuals: Chapter 7 and Chapter 13.

CHAPTER 7 – LIQUIDATION

Chapter 7 of the United States Federal Bankruptcy code addresses bankruptcy situations where the filer has little or no assets to speak of. If the Smith family were in this situation, they likely would have racked up a staggering amount of debt, whether it is credit card debt, medical bills, student loans, mortgage debt, tax liens or some combination of all of these. Chapter 7 filers are primarily asking the court to intercede on their behalf and prevent creditors from harassing them for payment on their bills. It would allow the Smiths the ability to simply walk away from their bills by selling what little assets they may have and paying off the creditors in a limited amount with whatever monies are generated from the asset sales.

Before one would apply to file Chapter 7 bankruptcy, a two part test is applied to determine if the debtor qualifies for this protection.[37]

- Ability to Repay – debtor's income is examined under a formula exempting necessary expenses required to subsist, such as food and rent to determine if the debtor will be able to repay at least 25% of the "non-priority unsecured debt" (credit cards and other consumer debt)
- Comparison to State Median Income

If the debtor earns in excess of the state's median income and is able to repay 25% of the non-priority debt, they will be prevented from filing Chapter 7 bankruptcy and must proceed under Chapter 13, Reorganization Bankruptcy.

If the Smith's were to meet the two criteria listed above, they would be granted an "automatic stay"; that is, court

---

37 www.expertlaw.com/library/bankruptcy/chapter_7_bankruptcy.
    html

granted protection effective immediately, which prevents creditors from collecting their respective debts which were in existence prior to bankruptcy filing. Any new debts incurred after the filing date would be payable to creditors. At this point a creditor is prevented from repossessing the Smith's car(s), foreclosing on their home, shutting off their electricity, garnishing their wages or taking any other extraordinary measures to collect what was owed them.

Once the Smiths are granted the automatic stay, a trustee will be appointed by the court to oversee the sale of most of their assets, with the objective of paying creditors as much of what they are owed as possible. Assets are separated into two categories, "exempt" and "non-exempt." The rationale is that the Smith's will still need some mode of transportation to allow them to get to work, so they may be able to retain some monies to buy an inexpensive car (read a Chevy not a Porsche). They will be allowed to keep some money to be able to pay rent for an apartment, and will be allowed to keep some of their clothes (no *St. John* evening gowns in all likelihood) and other bare essentials. The creditors will then line up to collect whatever proceeds result from the sale of the non-exempt assets, based on whether they are secured or unsecured creditors. A secured creditor is one who has a "security interest" in the property; meaning that their original loan was backed by collateral – the usual assets in this case are cars and homes. Unsecured creditors have no security interest in the debtor's property. Credit card debt is the most common type of unsecured debt.

DOES CHAPTER 7 EXONERATE ME FROM ALL DEBTS?

Chapter 7 bankruptcy is not a "get out of jail free" card. Yes, the Smiths would be granted protection from creditors, so the harassing phone calls would stop. Yes, they would be allowed to keep some assets to get on with their lives and attempt to rebuild their finances. However, they would still be liable for certain debts which cannot be discharged: a) child support b) student loans c) all tax obligations d) and any damage awards due injured parties prior to the bankruptcy filing. In addition, if the Smiths went on a shopping spree for luxury goods or secured significant cash advances within 60 days of the bankruptcy petition, those debts in all likelihood would not be discharged by the court.

Again, bankruptcy filings of any sort should be considered a last resort. Think of the damage the Smiths will have done. Their credit score, which is their financial name and reputation is ruined. It will take anywhere between 7-10 years to wipe the slate clean. This means that they will probably not be able to secure a mortgage unless they have someone cosign the loan. They will undoubtedly pay higher than market interest rates for any loans they are successful in obtaining since any lender will deem them to be a major credit risk. And they may even do significant psychological damage to themselves and their families. Even in 2011, declaring bankruptcy carries a stigma within our society. So who is most likely to file Chapter 7? Given that most of your assets will be sold to pay creditors off, this convention would most likely be used by those that have limited assets to their name, therefore a liquidation of few assets would not be so difficult for the filer. Young people and those who have not managed to acquire significant assets during their working careers and the frequently unemployed would be some of those individuals prone to file Chapter 7.

CHAPTER 13 – REORGANIZATION

It is not only those with limited assets and poor employment prospects who file bankruptcy. Sometimes, people have such little financial discipline that they become immersed in debt, purchasing anything and everything they desire until they reach the point where they are "in way over their heads" and unable to dig themselves out of the financial predicament they have created. These people may have good jobs, live in a nice home, drive nice cars, send their kids to good schools, take nice vacations. The trouble is, they are probably living way over their means.

Chapter 13 bankruptcy offers those who have a) had difficulty living within their means, b) been laid off for an extended period of time or c) wound up in financial distress by some other manner, the opportunity to take a court granted "time out", seek protection from their creditors, and with the help of a court appointed trustee, develop a plan to pay off their debts. One big assumption herein is that the filer has a solid source of income that will allow him to pay the debts with the help of some additional time. There are significant advantages to filing under this convention. In the Smiths case, it would allow them to keep their home and most of their assets. With the help of the trustee, they would be able to reschedule their secured debts and extend them over the life of the Chapter 13 plan. By extending the time needed to pay back their debts, the Smiths would have lower monthly payment which would enable them to live within their budget. The trustee acts as a loan consolidator, where he will accept payments from the filer, and distribute them to the respective creditors under a court approved plan.

CAN ANYONE FILE CHAPTER 13 BANKRUPTCY?

There are limitations to this bankruptcy convention. Should the Smiths have unsecured debts greater than $360,475 (at the time of this writing), or secured debts in excess of $1,081,400 (at the time of this writing), they would be prevented from filing Chapter 13 and would have to seek other recourse to protect themselves from creditors. Also, the Smiths would need to undergo court approved credit counseling before being allowed to seek protection in this fashion. Once these parameters have been met, the court grants an "automatic stay" to all creditor efforts similar to Chapter 7. The automatic stay can even stop a foreclosure already in process. Even though most creditors will receive full restitution from the filer, the damage done is similar to a Chapter 7 filing. The Smiths would see their credit rating destroyed for 7-10 years, affecting their ability to secure new mortgage and or other significant financing without the aid of a third party cosigner.

One note on Chapter 11 Bankruptcy: This book delves into the similarities and differences between Chapter 7 and Chapter 13 personal bankruptcy filings. Most individuals will have heard of Chapter 11 in the US Federal Bankruptcy Code. That section is typically used by corporations, although there may be instances when it applies to individuals. However, I cover bankruptcy in this book according to what typically occurs in our economy and not what may happen in every individual situation.

Summary / Tips to Remember

- Controlling spending is critical to maximizing disposable income and net worth – it is essential to understand the "root" causes of debt to keep one's spending habits in check
- Proper budgeting will allow a household to *accelerate* their way out of debt by ensuring that as one debt is retired, the same monthly amount goes to pay remaining debt balances!
- Obtaining an annual credit report allows a household to concentrate on eliminating all outstanding debt balances as well as protecting one's household against identity theft
- Every monthly payment obligation offers an opportunity for cost reduction; it may involve sacrifice and discipline, but *"short term pain, leads to long term gain!"*
- Personal bankruptcy is a last resort; if faced with this option, Chapter 7 (liquidation) and Chapter 13 offer households the opportunity for a fresh start, albeit with negative credit implications.

(H) HOME OWNERSHIP

The American dream is traditionally described in a way that portrays each household as owning their own home and, in essence, owning a piece of America. While this makes sense in principle, it should be done responsibly and only when an individual or a couple is *ready* for the actual commitment (the sub-prime mortgage crisis comes to mind). This is the third key pillar that I discuss in this handbook and I specifically place it after preparing a budget and eliminating debt because I believe there is a priority of recommended actions in the financial freedom chain. I would be naïve to imply that you must first eliminate all of your debt prior to entering into a contractual obligation to purchase a home. There should be a plan in place however, using a budget, that identifies the steps to eliminate one's debt position prior to buying a home.

The reason is that a mortgage will almost always be the largest monthly obligation for the average American, so the less outstanding debt you have prior to buying a home the better. In addition to the monthly payment, buying a home always entails the maintenance, repair, and general upkeep of the property, which can become a heavy financial burden. Should an individual enter into a home ownership agreement while being saddled with heavy consumer and other types of debt, it is possible that making the respective payments may prove too difficult to accomplish on a consistent basis. This may result in the repossession of your home or car by the corresponding lender, in the worst-case scenario.

WHEN IS THE RIGHT TIME TO BUY A HOME?

I believe a logical order exists to personal financial planning. First, one should adopt a sound budgeting philosophy that emphasizes living within or below one's means. To fully grasp this, understand that net pay will typically range between 65% - 70% of gross pay. This assumes participation in a tax deferred savings program (TDS), contribution to a medical plan to protect from sickness or ill health, and then honoring Federal, State, Local and FICA withholding taxes. At this point, one can determine within the total monthly bills, just how much money can be devoted to paying for a mortgage and all ancillary home-related costs. Ideally, by this time, all existing household debt will have been eliminated or reduced to manageable levels, since the monthly mortgage cost will most likely become the household's largest single monthly obligation.

Should the Smith family follow these steps, they will now be financially ready to take on this burden. However, there are other considerations that need to be addressed. First, I would suggest that before deciding on the purchase of a home, the Smith's should ask the following questions:

- Are their careers at a point where they are stable, or better yet, blossoming?
- Can they see themselves in one house for several years (4-5), so they don't lose money on re-sale?
- Do they like the city, the county or township, the various neighborhoods they currently live in?
- Are the school systems in the area of sufficiently high caliber?
- Is the crime rate in their area of interest low enough to be conducive to raising a family?
- Are their parks and other recreational opportunities nearby?

If their answers to these questions are affirmative, the Smith's should be ready to begin concentrating on the financial aspects of the purchase. Let's review some quick definitions prior to entering into a deeper dialogue:

Down Payment: A predetermined amount that a prospective buyer pays up front and is deducted from the total purchase (sale) price of a home. It is usually required to provide the lender (bank) with a degree of comfort that the rest of the mortgage or monthly payments will be made on time. This figure varies but a common minimum down payment has been equivalent to ~five percent of the sale price of the home[38]. After the sub-prime mortgage crisis, discussed in more detail further, it was not uncommon to see down payments rise to significantly higher percentages of the sale price of the property.

---

38   http://www.mortgagealmanac.com/articles/96-savingfordownpayment.html

Closing Costs: Additional one-time fees paid at the time of contract settlement when the title of the house is transferred to the new owner and the home buying process has closed. These costs include such items as attorney's fees, title insurance, number of days of interest payable until the first mortgage payment is due, home appraisals, etc...

Mortgage: The value of the loan the borrower (home-buyer) assumes. In essence, this amount equals the selling price of the home, plus the closing costs, minus the down payment. At settlement, the check the buyer presents to the seller will usually include the closing costs, so in essence, the mortgage will just be the selling price of the home, less the down payment.

Amortization: This refers to the schedule outlining the monthly breakdown of principal and interest payments due to the lender in equal installments. The schedule is structured in such a way that interest owed to the bank for the mortgage loan is paid down faster than the principal portion (the amount of money actually being borrowed) of the mortgage value. An abbreviated example is included at the end of this section.

Mortgages come in different forms, but they typically comprise two key components:

- **Fixed or Variable**: The loan type refers to the interest obligation within the loan. A fixed rate loan means that the interest rate is fixed for the life of the loan, usually fifteen or thirty years. This type of loan is recommended for most consumers even though the interest rate being assigned will likely be higher than other alternatives in the marketplace. In essence, it buys the consumer peace of mind, knowing that regardless of how high mortgage interest rates rise in the future due to market forces, the interest rate the borrower pays on a monthly basis will never change. In fact, this solution provides a win-win situation for most consumers, as their principal and interest payments are fixed, unless interest rates decrease substantially, presenting the opportunity to refinance their mortgage loan at lower market rates of interest.

Many consumers shop for lower interest rates than what fixed rate mortgages offer. A home selling for $100,000, will have a lower monthly payment the lower the interest rate becomes. Depending on the consumer's credit score as well as other pertinent financial information, the bank (lender) may offer a loan that, for a specific period of time (i.e., 1 – 5 years), will be less than the market value of prevailing fixed interest rate mortgages. This loan type is referred to as an *adjustable rate mortgage* (ARM), and it is **variable**, meaning that after an introductory period in which interest rates are fixed at a predetermined amount, the interest rate for the loan will fluctuate with market interest rates after the period specified in the loan agreement.

Obviously this represents a higher risk for the consumer even though a lower initial monthly payment (principal + interest) results. The uncertainty of a higher rate down the road is the risk. The reward, however, is a lower cash outlay at the beginning of the loan, allowing the consumer to either afford a more expensive home than otherwise might be the case, or to have greater disposable income for a myriad of uses. This type of loan might make sense for a young person or couple who anticipates a significant rise in income within a few years, or if the owner of the home only expects to live there for a few years.

- **Term**: The other key factor in the composition of the mortgage payment is the term of the loan. Although a mortgage can span many different periods, the two most common types are fifteen-year and thirty-year mortgages. First time homebuyers normally obtain thirty year financing because any term shorter than that will make it extremely difficult to afford the monthly payment obligation. Thirty year mortgages will carry higher interest rates than fifteen year mortgages, but the former will result in a lower total monthly payment, as will be discussed shortly, because the buyer has fifteen more years to pay off the home. As the household's income stream rises over time, owners may choose to obtain a lower interest rate and finance the remainder of the mortgage balance over fifteen years.

There are two schools of thought on this alternative: on the one hand, you will have a higher payment over fifteen years than if you financed the mortgage over thirty years at the same general level of interest rates, but at the end of that term, the property will be completely paid off and you will therefore have all that cash flow available for discretionary purposes. On the other hand, your cash flow over the first fifteen years will be mitigated, preventing you from using the extra cash for other purposes, such as investments, education funds for children, household repairs, and other discretionary purposes. The mortgage payment therefore, represents an opportunity cost to the consumer, since they can choose to use extra money to pay off the loan earlier, but will forgo the opportunity to use the extra monies to generate additional investment returns had they used that money to purchase stocks, bonds, mutual funds, exchange-traded funds (ETFs), other real estate, etc...

So much of an emphasis is made on saving for a down payment and the associated closing costs. **However, it is much more important to ensure that within your budget there is enough room to comfortably pay for the monthly mortgage payment.** Lenders (banks) often require a minimum down payment of 5 percent of the value of the home. While this is not a hard and fast rule, it is a fairly good guideline of what the marketplace requires. There have been times in the past, especially in the period between 2003 and 2007 that lenders provided incentives to buy a home with "no money down" but that was a sign of a very aggressive marketplace and did not necessarily represent the best solution for the buyer, as the incentive packages tended to be loaded with higher interest rates or other back-ended payment obligations. As with anything else, *read the fine print.*

Let's assume the Smiths are ready to enter into the home buying process. One of the very first things they need to do is take stock of their financial situation to determine if they are in a position to purchase a home. One way of doing this is by maintaining a personal balance sheet which details their household net worth.

PERSONAL BALANCE SHEET **Pre-Home Ownership**					
Assets			**Liabilities**		
Checking Accounts (Normal Balance)	$	2,500	Car Loan #1 (Balance Due Current Year)	$	2,500
Savings Accounts / CDs	S	15,000	Student Loan (Balance Due Current Year)	$	1,400
Money Market Accounts	$	500	Visa (Balance Due Current Year)*		
			Mastercard (Balance Due Current Year)*		
Tatal Current / Liquid Assets	**$**	**18,000**	**Total Current Liabilities**	**$**	**4,500**
Taxable Investment Accounts	$	12,500			
Tax Deferred Accounts (401k, 403b, IRA)	$	37,500	Car Loan #1 (Balance Due After Current Year)	$	14,400
Car #1 (Blue Book Value)	$	17,500	Student Loan (Balance Due After Current Year)	$	13,600
Car #2 (Blue Book Value)	$	1,800	Visa (Balance Due Current Year)	$	4,000
Jewelry / Other (Resale Value)	$	5,000	Mastercard (Balance Due Current Year)	$	2,500
Total Long Term / Non-liquid Assets	**$**	**74,,300**	**Total Long Term Liabilities**	**$**	**34,500**
Total Assets	**$**	**92,300**	**Total Liabilities**	**$**	**39,000**
			Smith Family Net Worth	**$**	**53,300**

* Assumes that when minimum payments are made, balance may increase after year 1 due to additional interest due.

For example purposes, let's assume they don't currently own a home, but instead rent their primary residence. This balance sheet tells us several things. First, assets (items owned) exceed liabilities (dollars owed), resulting in a positive net worth. Remember, the goal from a financial perspective should be to maximize one's personal net worth. The Smith's are off to a good start. Second, their jobs provide them with the necessary income to provide for their family as seen in the budget in Chapter 2. In addition, their liabilities remain manageable, with a car loan and student loans comprising well over 80% of their debt. The reason this is good is that those debts carry relatively low interest rates compared to credit card debt. Third, the Smith's are now embarking on an accelerated loan payment plan as described in Chapter 3. Therefore, this household is ready to begin augmenting their assets and the best way to do that at this point would be through the purchase of a primary residence.

Another critical step that needs to be taken at the beginning of the process is to request a credit report from any of the major credit rating agencies previously mentioned, Trans Union, Experian, and Equifax.[39] We know from Chapter 3 (Debt Elimination) that these companies maintain national databases that collect all of a household's credit history. The credit report will allow lenders to determine what kind of credit risk your household represents and what type of rate you may qualify for in purchasing a home. After you have checked with your bank and identified what rate of interest you qualify for, you are now ready to begin the home selection process. When beginning to house shop, beware of sticker shock. Home prices nationwide can rise at very steep rates from time to time, and certain highly desirable communities will experience exorbitant increases during a seller's market (e.g. 2003 – 2007 in the US). Do not let the sale price of a home instantly scare you. Instead, consult with your bank or real estate agent and have them calculate what your monthly payment will be to see if you can afford

---

39   http://www.transunion.com
http://www.equifax.com
http://www.experian.com

it within your budget. The monthly payment calculation may appear complicated at first, but it is simply a composition of four factors.

- **Principal (P)**: This is the portion of the monthly payment that directly reduces the remaining mortgage obligation of the home. If the value of the mortgage is $100,000 and your first payment consists of $200 worth of principal, you owe $99,800 on your home. Each dollar that is targeted for the principal portion of the loan increases a household's ownership or *equity* in the property. Equity is also known as net worth. Therefore, the more you pay of the principal, the greater the household's net worth. Every monthly mortgage payment includes a portion for the principal. This amount is dictated by the terms of the loan amortization schedule (a copy is included later in this chapter). If you wish to have a greater amount of principal paid each month, you can dedicate additional funds on top of your regular mortgage payment to pay down the principal more quickly (as long as your budget allows for it). This usually occurs if the homeowner decides to undertake an accelerated mortgage payment program, which I heartily recommend if you have the available funds.
- **Interest (I)**: This is the portion of the payment devoted to paying back the bank for the loan they created, allowing you to live in the house. This portion of the payment is tax deductible and is one of the primary reasons why individuals should

purchase a home as soon as they can rather than continue renting. Tax deductible means that the amount in question is "deducted" from your taxable income. It does not mean that the amount in question is somehow returned to you by the Federal government.

In the early years of the mortgage term, the interest constitutes the large majority of the monthly payment, as the obligation is designed to pay the bank before increasing your ownership (equity) in the house. This payment structure is referred to as the loan amortization. It works the same way with car loans; however, the key difference is that car loan interest is not tax deductible.

- **Taxes (T):** The third component of the monthly payment is dedicated to paying the real estate or personal property taxes the local government charges the property owner for the privilege of using the land the house sits on. This amount is typically based on the total assessed value of the property and tends to rise and fall depending on how expensive the real estate is considered. For example, property taxes in New York City are much higher on a per acre basis than those in Lansing, Michigan. This is due to supply and demand factors which determine how expensive a particular piece of property will be, given the demand of homeowners wanting to live in that particular city, county, municipality, etc....

Property taxes are generally tax deductible, similar to the interest payable on the mortgage. However, this component is not part of the loan amortization schedule, since it does not directly contribute to the payment of the mortgage. The local jurisdiction assessing this tax invoices the homeowner, typically twice a year, either directly or through the insurance company covering the property. Each month, when the homeowner pays the mortgage, the portion corresponding to the payment of the property tax is held in an escrow account, which accumulates the taxes paid until such time the local government entity remits its invoice for the taxes due. The principal drawback to rising home prices is that as the value of the home goes up, so does the assessed value of the property. Many homeowners who expect a fixed monthly mortgage payment for the life of their loan are often surprised when they learn their actual monthly payment is now higher even though their loan value and terms have not changed. The fact that their net worth has increased is often of secondary import to them, since this additional wealth can only be realized upon the sale of the house.

- **Insurance (I)**: The final and usually the smallest component of the monthly mortgage payment, is dedicated to satisfying the annual home owner's insurance on the property. Similar to property taxes, the amount designated for insurance coverage is held in escrow (set aside) until the insurance company remits an invoice once or twice per year. Mortgage lenders require borrowers to obtain a homeowner's insurance policy as a means of protecting their loans. Since the insurance industry is regulated by state commissions, availability and affordability of homeowner's insurance varies among states.[40] Homeowner's insurance protects homeowners from damages to their home that are sustained from bad weather, tornados, fire, and similar casualty losses. It also protects them from potential liabilities that occur on their property—a neighbor's child who falls on the driveway, for instance. Flood insurance, however, is sold as a separate policy because of its very high cost. Most homeowners typically do not have this coverage as part of their basic policy and often become very upset when basement flooding, due to heavy rains, is not covered under their policy. Since insurance companies find it very hard to make a profit on selling flood insurance due to its incredibly destructive nature, they leave it to the Federal government to sell this policy in many cases.

In the past, a fifth component has often been part of the monthly mortgage payment. This portion satisfies the **primary mortgage interest (PMI)** requirement. In certain cases, lenders will request that prospective buyers meet very stringent down-payment thresholds, sometimes as much as 20% of the value of the home. If the buyer cannot meet this requirement, the lender will impose an additional cost on the mortgage to cover the lender for the perceived additional risk their company is assuming by issuing a mortgage to the prospective buyer. PMI is not applied consistently, but is

---

40   http://www.netquote.com/Default.aspx?ProductCategory=Home &nqid=10076&status=home+owner+insurance

a potential cost buyers should consider when determining whether to purchase a home.

As you prepare your household budget, you need to gauge how much of an impact the monthly mortgage payment will make on your total budget. There are two rules of thumb that you will hear from time to time:

- **30 percent rule** - the monthly mortgage payment should not exceed 30 percent of the total monthly household *gross* income.[41]
- **36 percent rule** — the total monthly household debt/gross income ratio should not exceed 36 percent.[42]

These guidelines, which are not mandatory, exist to protect both the buyer and the lender. The buyer needs to ensure she does not wind up in a situation where an inordinate amount of salary / income is devoted to paying the monthly mortgage, and that the resources are available to handle all other monthly obligations. In essence you want to avoid becoming *"house poor"*. The bank also wants to prevent a situation where individuals are granted loans which they will be unable to repay. Once you have qualified for the loan and selected a home to live in, make sure that the funds you are dedicating to servicing the monthly payment (P/I/T/I) are augmented by some amount that is dedicated toward home emergencies. It is important

---

41   http://www.hud.gov/offices/cpd/affordablehousing/

42   http://cgi.money.cnn.com/tools/houseafford/houseafford.html

to realize that homes require constant maintenance and upkeep. Unless you or someone in your household is especially handy, it is important that your monthly budget include a "maintenance reserve" line item. From leaky faucets and problematic toilets to malfunctioning garage door openers and furnace disruptions, experts feel that an annual maintenance budget of ~1% of the purchase price of the home should cover most of the run-of-the-mill problems that crop up.[43]

I have mentioned some of the costs that can arise in the process of buying and owning a home. However, Americans should keep in mind that for the vast majority of homeowners, their house will be the greatest asset in their net worth calculation. As I mentioned previously, home prices can rise steeply in certain periods of economic activity, although there are periods where home values remain stagnant or can even fall significantly. In a free market economy and over the long term, though, home prices should appreciate, especially if improvements are made that maintain and increase the value of the property. The following diagram shows the average appreciation of home prices from 1991 to 2001. This should not be taken as an indication of any future guarantees, but it should serve merely to allow the prospective buyer to understand what gains are possible in their net worth over time.[44]

---

43   http://www.vertex42.com/ExcelTemplates/home-expense-calculator.html

44   http://www.realestateabc.com/graphs/natlmedian.htm

US Median Home Price Appreciation 1989 - 2004	
1 Year	2.8%
3 Year	3.7%
5 Year	3.7%
10 Year	4.1%
15 Year	5.0%

Please keep in mind that these figures represent compounded annual rates of growth. For example, if a home was purchased in 1991 for $100,000, that same home in 2001, might have reflected a current market value of $152,350. Assuming that the homeowner would have been making payment on that same home for the entire ten years, the homeowner's net worth in the property will have grown by approximately $65 to $75K, depending on how much principal would have been paid during those same ten years. Compounding rates of interest are an incredible and completely misunderstood source of potential wealth creation, and this will be discussed in much more detail in the next chapter. One other financial homeowner consideration I would like to elaborate on is the concept of home equity loans and home equity lines of credit (HELOC). Simple definitions are provided below:

Home Equity Loan: A **fixed rate** loan secured by one's primary residence or second home. Typically issued in one lump sum, this loan can be for amounts ranging all the way up to most of the equity (ownership) the homeowner has in their home. Home equity is calculated by subtracting the amount of debt left in the mortgage loan from the fair market value of the home.[45] Most lenders will require that the homeowner have at least some minimum amount of equity in the home before they will issue a home equity loan, since the borrower is accessing money at lower interest rates than they would otherwise be able to do so.

Home Equity Line of Credit: a loan that enables a consumer to use the value of a home minus what is owed on the home. A home equity line of credit may also allow a consumer to consolidate other higher interest loans, such as credit cards.[46] The key difference with respect to a home equity loan is that the line of credit represents funds available to draw from, at **variable rates** of interest, since monies are being borrowed at different periods of time, when interest rates may differ from previous withdrawals from a line of credit.

Remember that as each mortgage payment is made, the total principal owed on the property is reduced, adding to the net worth or equity of the homeowner (see the amortization schedule below). An equity loan or a HELOC is a way for the homeowner to raise immediate cash for significant payments that might be coming due, with the promise they will be repaid with interest, restoring the full equity value of the property. For example, the homeowner may need to pay for college tuition for children, or a wedding, or the homeowner might wish to consolidate and pay off several credit card balances. This might be a very good idea given that the interest on home equity loans is generally much lower than

---

45   http://www.investorwords.com/5605/home_equity.html
46   http://www.investorwords.com/5606/home_equity_line_of_credit.html

consumer credit, and the interest portion of home equity loans and HELOCs is tax deductible.

Unfortunately, many times consumers use these loan instruments as a way of raising quick cash, reducing the equity value of their homes for luxury or discretionary purposes. Sometimes they are also used as methods to build up emergency funds. While the use of these loans makes sense instead of obtaining consumer loans at much higher interest rates, it overshadows a larger issue which is, *if you don't need the item, don't borrow the money.* First of all, it can show poor fiscal budgeting skills when you are unable to save through the monthly budgeting process. It indicates that your level of spending may be too high for a variety of reasons. Discretionary purchases should come from savings generated and accumulated each month (disposable income). Secondly, if you are using a home equity loan to build up cash savings, think again. Even though there is a tax deductible characteristic to these loans, the homeowner will generally still pay out rates of interest in excess of what they are able to save in a simple savings account where the emergency funds are stored. Although these instruments are valuable tools if used correctly, they should not be used as ways to raise quick cash for non-emergency purposes!

MONTHLY MORTGAGE – SEPARATING PRINCIPAL FROM INTEREST

Now that we have identified the key components of the monthly mortgage payment, we need to understand how the bank's portion of the mortgage proceeds is structured. When a lender provides the borrower with funds to purchase any big ticket item, that loan is accompanied by a corresponding interest rate that helps the lender cover its operating costs, default risk, profit requirements and its opportunity cost of not placing those funds in alternative investments. In the case of a mortgage, where the lender issues a fixed rate loan to the borrower, the monthly payment obligation to the bank (P / I) will be the same each month for the entire life of the loan, and will be comprised of a principal component and an interest component, whose values will rise (principal) and fall (interest) each month, while keeping the total amount of P&I fixed each month.

The monthly change between principal and interest amounts is referred to as the loan's amortization, and it essentially reflects the fact that the lender (bank) structures the loan to receive the interest payments first before the borrower pays down the principal portion. The remaining principal balance from the bank's perspective reflects the balance owed on the mortgage. For the consumer, the total cumulative principal paid on the loan at any given time reflects his ownership stake in the property, assuming the current value of the home equals the sales price. If the value of the home > sales price, the difference is additional equity to the homeowner. If the current value of the home < sales price, that amount (referred to as being "under water") reflects a loss in the property to the homeowner, offsetting any equity gains made in paying down the principal balance. Below is a sample amortization schedule for the Smith's new home. It reflects mortgage payments consistent with the Smith Family Budget displayed in Chapter 2.

SAMPLE AMORTIZATION SCHEDULE

Mortgage Value	$ 237,500
Annual Rate	5.0%
Payments per Year	12
Total Monthly Payments	360
Principal / Interest	$ 1,270

Payment	Principal	Interest	Cum Principal	Cum Interest	Remaining Mortgage
1	$ 280.08	$ 989.58	$ 280.08	$ 989.58	$ 237,219.92
2	281.24	988.42	561.32	1,978.00	236,938.68
3	282.42	987.24	843.74	2,965.24	236,656.26
4	283.59	986.07	1,127.33	3,951.31	236,372.67
5	284.77	984.89	1,412.11	4,936.20	236,087.89
6	285.96	983.70	1,698.07	5,919.90	235,801.93
7	287.15	982.51	1,985.22	6,902.41	235,514.78
8	288.35	981.31	2,273.57	7,883.72	235,226.43
9	289.55	980.11	2,563.12	8,863.83	234,936.88
10	290.76	978.90	2,853.88	9,842.73	234,646.12
11	291.97	977.69	3,145.85	10,820.42	234,354.15
12	293.19	976.48	3,439.03	11,796.90	234,060.97
13	294.41	975.25	3,733.44	12,772.15	233,766.56
14	295.63	974.03	4,029.08	13,746.18	233,470.92
15	296.87	972.80	4,325.94	14,718.98	233,174.06
16	298.10	971.56	4,624.04	15,690.53	232,875.96
17	299.34	970.32	4,923.39	16,660.85	232,576.61
18	300.59	969.07	5,223.98	17,629.92	232,276.02
19	301.84	967.82	5,525.82	18,597.74	231,974.18
20	303.10	966.56	5,828.93	19,564.30	231,671.07
21	304.36	965.30	6,133.29	20,529.59	231,366.71
22	305.63	964.03	6,438.92	21,493.62	231,061.08
23	306.91	962.75	6,745.83	22,456.37	230,754.17
24	308.19	961.48	7,054.02	23,417.85	230,445.98
25	309.47	960.19	7,363.49	24,378.04	230,136.51
26	310.76	958.90	7,674.24	25,336.94	229,825.76
27	312.05	957.61	7,986.30	26,294.55	229,513.70
28	313.35	956.31	8,299.65	27,250.86	229,200.35
29	314.66	955.00	8,614.31	28,205.86	228,885.69
30	315.97	953.69	8,930.28	29,159.55	228,569.72
31	317.29	952.37	9,247.57	30,111.92	228,252.43
32	318.61	951.05	9,566.18	31,062.98	227,933.82
33	319.94	949.72	9,886.12	32,012.70	227,613.88
34	321.27	948.39	10,207.39	32,961.09	227,292.61
35	322.61	947.05	10,529.99	33,908.14	226,970.01
36	323.95	945.71	10,853.95	34,853.85	226,646.05

The Smith family's amortization schedule encompasses the first three years of a thirty-year payment cycle, and includes the following assumptions:

Sale Price of Property = $250,000

Down-payment = $12,500 (5%)

Closing Costs = $5,000 (2.0%)

The payment cycle breaks down the principal and interest portion. Recall that the taxes and insurance are not reflected in the amortization schedule because they are directed at fulfilling state and county obligations (taxes) and property protection (insurance). **The combination of principal and interest results in the same monthly total of $1,270** and will remain fixed throughout the life of the loan as long as it is a **fixed rate** mortgage. However, the portion that is principal grows slightly each month and the corresponding interest decreases slightly every month. The following process details how the amortization works:

Step 1: Convert the mortgage interest rate into a monthly "factor" (Rate / 12)
Step 2: Multiply the "factor" in Step 1 by "Remaining Mortgage Balance" – this is the *Interest* portion
Step 3: Subtract the *Interest* portion from the total P&I of $1,270 – this is the *Principal* portion
Step 4: Repeat Steps 1 – 3 for the entire life of the loan

The bottom line is that **after each payment, the household's net worth increases** at the same time that greater tax deductibility is achieved with the accumulating interest payments. Over the course of many years, the tax deductibility advantage is slowly reduced as greater portions of the monthly payment are targeted at the principal, which is not tax deductible. However, the result is a net worth balance that increases at a slightly greater rate each month.

The basic point to take away from this chapter is that every day that you rent, you lose from a financial perspective. Some may disagree, but from a net worth standpoint as well as from a tax filing standpoint, it is hard to argue that renting your primary home can improve your financial position, especially over a protracted time horizon. This is not to say that you need to run out and purchase a primary residence immediately. The process must be conducted judiciously, by first determining how expensive a house you can afford and studying the neighborhood in question to understand if the location will present long-term growth prospects. For example, you want to avoid buying a home in neighborhoods with higher crime rates than average or underperforming public school systems. From a resale standpoint, no one will want to pay you the amount you feel your house is worth. You may also decide to delay the home purchase temporarily if you recently moved to an area because of a job offer. You and your spouse may want to first convince yourself that the neighborhood you live in is one which will bring you long-term satisfaction. You must take into account your current financial status as well as your long-term goals and objectives prior to making the decision which will likely end up being the greatest financial asset in your portfolio.

We will end this chapter by re-visiting the Smith's household *Balance Sheet*, now that they have purchased their new home.

PERSONAL BALANCE SHEET				
Home Ownership				
Assets		**Liabilities**		
Checking Accounts (Normal Balance)	$ 2,500	Car Loan #1 (Balance Due Current Year)	$	3,100
		Student Loan (Balance Due Current Year)	$	1,400
		3225 Maple Road (short term)	$	3,439
		Visa & Mastercard (Balance Due Current Year)*		
Tatal Current / Liquid Assets	**$ 2,500**	**Total Current Liabilities**	**$**	**7,939**
3225 Maple Road	$ 250,000			
Taxable Investment Accounts	$ 12,500	3225 Maple Road (long term)	$	234,061
Tax Deferred Accounts (401k, 403b, IRA)	$ 37,500	Car Loan #1 (Balance Due After Current Year)	$	14,400
Car #1 (Blue Book Value)	$ 17,500	Student Loan (Balance Due After Current Year)	$	13,600
Car #2 (Blue Book Value)	$ 1,800	Visa (Balance Due Current Year)	$	4,000
Jewelry / Other (Resale Value)	$ 5,000	Mastercard (Balance Due Current Year)	$	2,500
Total Long Term / Non-liquid Assets	**$ 324,300**	**Total Long Term Liabilities**	**$**	**268,561**
Total Assets	**$ 326,800**			
		Smith Family Net Worth	**$**	**50,300**

As you can see, the example shows that immediately after the purchase of the home, the Smith's net worth actually decreases slightly. This is due to the fact that their savings and money market accounts were depleted in order to pay for the down-payment and closing costs. This reduction will likely be temporary, as their equity in the home (net worth) will begin to increase after each monthly payment. The mechanics of this increase will be driven more by a reduction in liabilities (with each mortgage payment, you will owe *less* principal on the house) than it will by an increase in assets. The assets will only increase from the $250K reflected in the balance sheet, if the value of the home rises over time due to supply and demand as well as inflationary factors. If the value of the home should decrease from the original purchase price, as was the case with many homes purchased from 2005 – 2009, the household net worth would actually decrease.

A better measure of the Smith's net worth might be taken three years after the initial purchase:

PERSONAL BALANCE SHEET Home Ownership (3 Yrs Post Purchase)				
Assets			**Liabilities**	
Checking Accounts (Normal Balance)	$ 2,500		Car Loan #1 (Balance Due Current Year)	$ 3,855
Savings Accounts	$ 5,000		Student Loan (Balance Due Current Year)	$ 4,773
			3225 Maple Road (short term)	$ 3,800
			Visa & Mastercard (Balance Due Current Year)*	
Tatal Current / Liquid Assets	**$ 7,500**		**Total Current Liabilities**	**$ 12,428**
3225 Maple Road	$ 283,657			
Taxable Investment Accounts	$ 14,470		3225 Maple Road (long term)	$ 222,846
Tax Deferred Accounts (401k, 403b, IRA)	$ 43,411		Car Loan #1 (Balance Due After Current Year)	$ 1,748
Car #1 (Blue Book Value)	$ 14,250		Student Loan (Balance Due After Current Year)	
Car #2 (Blue Book Value)	$ 650		Visa (Balance Due Current Year)	*Paid off*
Jewelry / Other (Resale Value)	$ 5,000		Mastercard (Balance Due Current Year)	*Paid off*
Total Long Term / Non-liquid Assets	**$ 361,438**		**Total Long Term Liabilities**	**$ 224,594**
Total Assets	**$ 368,938**			
			Smith Family Net Worth	**$ 131,916**

In just three years, the Smith's net worth has more than doubled from ~$50K to ~ $132K. Several financial milestones have been met and other assumptions have been made as discussed below:

- Credit cards, student loans and car loans reflect the accelerated debt repayment plan from Ch - 3
- The home value assumes a conservative historical growth rate of 4.3% compounded annually

- Taxable / tax deferred accounts assume a conservative growth rate of 5% compounded annually
- A savings account reflects the build-up of a rainy day fund using disposable income
- Car values reflect continuing depreciation of the vehicles

Summary / Tips to Remember

- Over the long term, from a financial perspective, "everyday you rent you lose"
  - o Every mortgage payment increases your equity stake in the house as well as your household net worth (assets are rising and liabilities are falling)
  - o Historically, home prices rise over the long run somewhere between 4% – 6% annually; every dollar of home value appreciation above the mortgage amount results in an increase in the owner's net worth
  - o Every dollar paid in mortgage interest *(I)* and property taxes *(T)* is tax deductible; that is, it reduces your taxable income dollar for dollar
  - o The equity in your home allows you to be eligible to take out Home Equity Loans or Home Equity Lines of Credit for large home improvements; the upside is that interest on these instruments is also tax deductible and these loans typically carry below market interest rates; the downside is that you are borrowing against your own net worth, and are increasing your total liabilities.

- Buy a home as soon as you are ready to make the commitment, which means in essence that you have reached a level of stability in your chosen profession; it also assumes you have reduced your debt to a manageable level
- Mortgages should be drawn at fixed rates even though they will carry slightly higher interest rates; Adjustable Rate mortgages should only be drawn if you expect to receive a large step-up in income in the near future (i.e. you are graduating from school in the short to intermediate term and expect significant remuneration as a result)
- I would recommend *accelerating* your mortgage payoff timetable. By paying the mortgage bi-weekly instead of monthly, or by paying the next month's principal with each monthly mortgage payment, you will shave off years from your total obligation as well as many thousands of dollars in interest costs. This should provide a household with peace of mind and significant options.
  - Caution: a school of thought exists that believe you should carry a mortgage balance as long as possible to provide one with interest cost deductibility as well as additional funds to invest with opportunities for greater percentage rates of return.

(I) INVESTING

More and more Americans below the age of fifty have serious doubts as to whether they will be able to afford retirement. After all, fewer companies each day are offering employee pensions that would guarantee a *defined benefit* for their retirement based on their years of service in a particular company. In addition, they view Social Security as a system which will eventually collapse under its own weight and become bankrupt. Many people are resigned to the fact that they will work well into their seventies, or in some cases for the rest of their lives, since they will not have enough money coming to them from Social Security to provide for their needs and desires in their golden years. In 2004, the retirement age for Social Security benefits had already risen to sixty-seven from sixty-five for those individuals born after 1960.[47] Although I personally believe the system is in deep trouble and requires a complete overhaul, I do think that there will be a system resembling what Social Security appears like today, perhaps with some private investment options that will be available to assist senior citizens when they retire.

---

47   http://www.ssa.gov/retirechartred.htm

The key is to prepare for your financial future without assuming that Social Security will be there as the retirement safety net. Much of the anxiety caused by the fear that Social Security will not exist, could be avoided with careful planning, discipline, and by investing in one's own retirement at an early age. Investing comprises the fourth pillar of what I refer to as the six major cornerstones of your personal financial health. After a household's primary residence, investments are usually the next largest asset class in one's personal balance sheet. Let's once again re-visit the balance sheet for the Smith family.

PERSONAL BALANCE SHEET Home Ownership (3 Yrs Post Purchase)					
Assets			**Liabilities**		
Checking Accounts (Normal Balance)	$	2,500	Car Loan #1 (Balance Due Current Year)	$	3,855
Savings Accounts	$	5,000	Student Loan (Balance Due Current Year)	$	4,773
			3225 Maple Road (short term)	$	3,800
			Visa & Mastercard (Balance Due Current Year)*		
Tatal Current / Liquid Assets	**$**	**7,500**	**Total Current Liabilities**	**$**	**12,428**
3225 Maple Road		$ 283,657			
Taxable Investment Accounts	$	14,470	3225 Maple Road (long term)	$	222,846
Tax Deferred Accounts (401k, 403b, IRA)	$	43,411	Car Loan #1 (Balance Due After Current Year)	$	1,748
Car #1 (Blue Book Value)	$	14,250	Student Loan (Balance Due After Current Year)		
Car #2 (Blue Book Value)	$	650	Visa (Balance Due Current Year)		Paid off
Jewelry / Other (Resale Value)	$	5,000	Mastercard (Balance Due Current Year)		Paid off
Total Long Term / Non-liquid Assets		**$ 361,438**	**Total Long Term Liabilities**		**$ 224,594**
Total Assets		**$ 368,938**			
			Smith Family Net Worth		**$ 131,916**

As you can see, a personal balance sheet, much like a corporate statement of financial position, comprises the three basic categories: assets (items owned), liabilities (items owed), and net worth (remainder). Assets and liabilities are both segregated into current and long-term categories. From a corporate standpoint, one year usually represents the demarcation between current and long-term. From a household standpoint, the difference is less concrete, but current assets are usually those which can be turned into cash fairly quickly, while long-term assets take more time to convert into cash. On the liability side, "current" refers to those obligations which are due in fairly short order (i.e., 1 year), while the long-term category is reserved for those items which come due at a later point in time.

BALANCE SHEET – ITEMS OF NOTE:

- Primary residences (3225 Maple Road in the example above) and other real estate, which may or may not be subjected to mortgages (depending on whether the loans have been paid in full), constitute assets, whereas renting your house or apartment is never considered an asset that contributes to your household's net worth. This is a clear representation of the old adage that says, "**Every day you rent, you lose**," because you are never building an ownership position.

- Although the re-sale value of the cars on the asset side exceeds the amount owed for each vehicle, please note that this is only due to accelerated debt repayment plans adopted in the Debt Elimination chapter. The key point is that although cars are assets, they rarely increase in value (unless you own an antique), and are actually **depreciable** assets, meaning they lose their value as time progresses. Many people spend very large sums of money on automobiles, but by and large, **they do little more than provide a status symbol for a household since they do virtually nothing to increase your net worth**, and in fact may contribute significantly to a cash flow reduction the more expensive the car.

- Notice that car loans, student loans, and the "current" portion of the mortgage constitute three different liabilities for this family. If the number of total debt obligations increases substantially through additional borrowing on credit cards and other items, debt consolidation at one low interest rate is an avenue worth exploring. **If the debt consolidation alternative is ever pursued, please note that it may have negative short term ramifications to one's credit report, since lenders may view that decision to be made out of concern for rising debt totals.**

- Notice that current assets are < current liabilities. The inference is that the cash assets are not quite sufficient to cover the short-term obligations (bills coming due in less than one year). In the Smith's situation, it does not represent much of a concern because their household budget shows that the sum total of all debt obligations can be handled comfortably based on the combined level of income for Mr. and Mrs. Smith. However, in certain cases, this difference could pose a major problem to the individual household and may require immediate attention, since the concern might exist that the household is unable to pay bills as they come due.

Since investing is a key contributor to household net worth, we need to understand what opportunities are available for each household. To reiterate, it is critical to first establish and maintain a budget to prioritize your household obligations. Pay off most or all of your debt balances as quickly as possible and then attempt to purchase a home that you can afford vis a vis your budget, as that will most likely be your household's greatest asset and it offers the tax advantages discussed in the previous chapter.

Many people believe they should begin investing immediately. I agree with this in certain situations. Many companies offer tax-deferred savings plans to employees (401k, 403b), which will be discussed later on in this chapter. Those people working for themselves or for companies that do not offer these tax deferred savings plans can participate in IRAs (Individual Retirement Accounts). All individuals should participate in any of these vehicles as soon as they are eligible since monies are able to grow, on a **tax deferred** basis, at compounding rates of interest for decades before the government begins to tax those funds.

Where mistakes are made however, are in those instances where individuals might wish to invest portions of their monthly *disposable* income in **taxable** instruments, such as stocks and bonds, while still carrying significant consumer debt (e.g. credit cards) burdens which are subject to excessive interest rates. For example, credit card rates sport average annual rates somewhere in the low- to mid-double-digits, while the average annual savings rate or stock market returns range from the low-to-high single digits. This will always result in a money-losing proposition, because you are earning less money in savings than is owed in interest obligations. **Bottom line: Attempt to pay down most of the** non-mortgage debt, particularly high interest bearing consumer debt, prior to committing funds in taxable investments.

The basic goal of any investment is to set aside money with the goal of having that investment grow over time. One key principle of investing not understood by many investors is the power of a **compound rate of interest** that, when applied correctly, allows investors to generate many times the income they would ordinarily expect. Below is a specific example that shows the effects of compounding interest rates. If $20,000 is invested at a 5% **compounded** annual rate of interest over three years, compared to investing the same $20,000 at a 5% **simple** interest rate with no annual compounding, the end result will be .7 % greater using compounded interest rates.

SIMPLE vs COMPOUND INTEREST

Interest	Rate	Investment	Total Value Yr 1	Total Value Yr 2	Total Value Yr 3
Simple	5.0%	$ 20,000	$ 21,000	$ 22,000	$ 23,000
Compound	5.0%	$ 20,000	$ 21,000	$ 22,050	$ 23,153

Imagine if the principal involved was larger and the amount invested occurred every month through a tax-deferred savings account such as a 401k plan over a period of twenty-five to thirty years. The additional earning power would be significantly greater. This describes the wealth generating opportunities using any type of invested account.

The key point here is to take advantage of employee sponsored tax-deferred savings accounts as early in one's working career as possible. If $1,000 is invested each month for a period of twenty years generating an average compounded annual rate of return of 7 percent over that period, the end result would be $520,927. If this same amount were to be invested over a ten-year period with the same expected rate of return, the total amount of the account would be only $173,085. By beginning the investing process ten years earlier, the investor is able to generate 3X the amount. Another way to look at this is that using that same time horizon of ten years and the same expected annual rate of return of 7 percent, the investor would have to save $2,978 monthly instead of $1,000 in order to make a roughly similar total.

DON'T ALL INVESTMENT OPPORTUNITIES OFFER COMPOUND INTEREST RATES?

Unfortunately, certain investments do not afford investors with the opportunity to grow returns in a compounded fashion. Bonds are the clearest example of this, since they offer investment income as a flat percentage of the initial investment. Stocks on the other hand do afford investors this opportunity, but are typically accompanied by higher risk levels, exemplified by a greater standard deviation of expected rates of return (RoR). Inflation has the ability to erode a household's future investment returns because those interest rates are compounded, so it behooves an investor to implement an asset growth strategy that drives much of its future earnings power from compounded interest growth, to help offset the earnings erosion that inflation will drive.

Every investment decision comes down to a simple question: What level of risk is the consumer willing to undertake? Stocks, on average, have slightly higher risk than other traditional investment alternatives such as real estate, bonds, and precious metals. However, since stocks are essentially betting on the future earnings growth of a company, they will be able to share in those profits to a greater degree than bonds. Thus, they provide greater potential for reward, offset by a higher level of risk being assumed. While this book is not meant to serve as an investment guide, I will describe some of these more common investment alternatives available to consumers.

Investment Options
Stocks

Many companies try to raise money in the public marketplace by issuing shares of stock in their companies. Firms raise money in order to finance their expansion, hopefully resulting in additional revenue and profit growth. These shares of stock equate to ownership in the company. For example, if a company has 1,000,000 shares of stock outstanding in the marketplace, and an individual, or an institution (i.e. mutual fund), purchases 10,000 shares of the outstanding stock, they would enjoy a 1 percent ownership of that company.

Shareholders typically raise their net worth from stock ownership in two ways: stock price appreciation and dividends. Many of us have heard the adage "Buy low, sell high!" This is what stock price appreciation means. If you purchase one share of stock in XYZ Corporation at $25, and in twelve months the price rises to $30, you will have made a **paper** profit of $5 on that share of stock and generated a 20 percent return in one year (before taxes and sales commissions). A paper profit indicates the individual has not sold the stock, but the value of the holding has increased. Only upon sale will the profit be **realized**. The price of a common stock represents a "claim" by investors on the **future** earnings of the company. The price of a stock will increase if enough investors believe that the company's operating activities will drive sufficient future earnings (profits) in the company to warrant their investment in the stock.

Dividends are the second way a shareholder typically increases his value. These payments are not guaranteed but represent periodic (usually quarterly) disbursements from companies out of the total earnings (net income) generated by their operations. Companies make these payments to reward shareholders for their decision to invest in the company's future. Once that potential is realized, companies use dividends to retain current investors and to entice potential investors by convincing them that future prospects remain bright for continued earnings growth. Although the payments are not guaranteed, once firms declare a dividend for the first time, they are very reluctant to discontinue these payments, because the lack of or reduction in a dividend will indicate that the company's operations may be suffering.

Many companies issue two types of stock: **common** and **preferred**. There are several differences between the two types, but some of the major differences lie in the dividend payment order and the total dividend amount paid per share. Preferred stockholders are guaranteed dividend payments and receive those dividends prior to common stockholders, at such time the company issues the quarterly payments. Preferred stockholders often are paid a higher amount relative to the value of the share price than are common stockholders (this is known as the **dividend yield**). If the company suffers a particularly poor quarter or if the prospects for future earnings growth are very poor, and the company only has a certain amount of dividend dollars available for payment, they need to pay the preferred stockholders their expected amount and either skip the quarterly payment to the common stockholders or pay them a reduced amount than what has been the previously declared dividend payment.

Most shareholders, however, opt for common stock because even though the dividend payments are not guaranteed, the potential for share price appreciation is usually greater. The reason is explained by a risk/reward rationale. Usually, fewer preferred stock shares are available for trading, compared to common stock. This could be because the company may be reluctant to issue additional shares which guarantee a higher dividend payment than other shares trading in the open market, such as common stock. If investors feel there is a good opportunity for earnings growth in the company, they will be attracted to buy the common stock. While dividends are good reasons to buy the stock, more significant money-making potential lies in the opportunity for the price of the stock to rise. The price of the stock rises when more people want to buy the stock than there are people willing to sell. The price rises until a point is reached where the number of buyers equals the number of sellers. This is a classic example of supply and demand. On the other hand, since there are fewer people vying for a company's preferred stock shares (due to fewer shares outstanding in the marketplace), the chances of sharp movements up or down in the preferred stock price are significantly less than common stock.

Stock is often the means that companies initially use to finance their growth objectives, marking the transfer from a private (no public ownership) to a public company. Firms typically do not resort to the stock (equity) market for financing very often, opting instead to have their internal operations fund their growth as repeated issuances of stock can tend to cheapen (dilute) the value of the shares already outstanding in the marketplace. You will often hear the term IPO, which stands for **initial public offering**. This marks the first time a company issues stock and is usually characterized by an initial appreciation in the value of the company, as the public tends to get excited about future earnings growth potential.

One point worth mentioning is that much of the time that individuals engage in the buying and selling of stocks and bonds, the transaction is usually taxable (unless done within a tax-deferred vehicle such as an IRA, as we will discuss later) at such time that the individual sells the asset, if a profit has been generated as a result of the sale. If the investor has held the common stock for more than 1 year prior to the sale, the profit will be taxed at 15%, the current long term capital gains rate. If the asset was held for less than one year, the profit (short term capital gain) will be taxed at the ordinary income rate for that investor, equivalent to the investor's current income tax bracket, which we will discuss in more detail in the Tax chapter[48].

Stocks are the most popular investment vehicle for Americans, who either purchase them individually or through mutual funds. In fact, in 2011, over 50% of all American households, or more than 57 million homes, owned stocks through mutual fund shares, up from 5% of households in 1980.[49] As recently as 2005, mutual fund shares comprised approximately 40% of an average household's financial assets.[50] There are a couple of reasons for this, in my estimation. First, stocks and/or mutual funds are easier to invest in than bonds for most Americans. If you want to purchase 100 shares of XYZ Company or 100 shares of ABCDF mutual fund, you simply call your broker (i.e. Charles Schwab, Merrill Lynch) or go on-line and complete the transaction, with a similar brokerage firm executing the trade. Bonds, which we will discuss in the next section, tend to be more confusing for the average investor, for various reasons. Real estate can also be quite involved, and precious metals are used by individuals largely as hedges against inflation, rather than for long-term investment results. Second, common stocks have provided greater investment returns than any other investment vehicle over most of the last cen-

---

48   http://www.ehow.com/info_7750323_tax-consequences-day-trading.html

49   http://www.gallup.com/poll/147206/stock-market-investments-lowest-1999.aspx

50   http://www.sec.gov/news/press/extra/seniors/usmutualfundownership.pdf

tury, averaging approximately 8% – 9% annual returns in that time frame.

Mutual Funds

Most Americans own their common stock in these investment vehicles. Mutual funds are baskets of individual stocks and bonds, lumped together in order to diversify (mitigate) an investor's risk. The purpose is not to have all of a household's financial "eggs" in one basket. The other key characteristic is that the funds are invested by a professional money manager with experience in the nuances of stock picking. For their services, investors are charged an annual fee, which is reflected as a percentage of the total value of the mutual fund. This is known as the *expense ratio* and comprises the management fee of the fund, the administrative costs of running the fund, marketing / distribution fees (a.k.a 12b-1 fees) and other operating costs of the fund[51]. The average expense ratio for an "actively managed" mutual fund has recently been documented to be in the range of 1.5%. That means that the fund will pay itself 1.5% of your total investment on an annual basis regardless of performance. This ratio has been trending upward over the last several years, meaning that it is costing you more and more in administrative fees to own a mutual fund.

Investors do not have to purchase actively managed mutual funds. They can reduce their costs of owning these funds substantially by investing in **index** funds. These are mutual funds that track the performance of a specific index

---

51   http://www.fool.com/school/mutualfunds/costs/ratios.htm

such as the S&P 500, the Russell 2000 index of small capi-
talization (smaller) companies, the NASDAQ index (more
technology oriented), etc… In addition, individuals can buy
index funds of foreign countries or regions as well. It should
be noted that the expense ratio covers all costs of running
the fund except for the up-front sales commission. This is
known as the **load** and please note that only a portion of
funds charge this fee. The load (sales commission) and the
12b-1 fees (marketing / advertising) frequently frustrate
investors because you are paying significant fees that have
nothing to do with the actual performance of the fund.

The principle with mutual funds is the same as it is
with any investment: "Buy low, sell high!" Every trading
day, the total number of shares a particular mutual fund
holds of each individual holding (stock, bond, etc..) is multiplied by the market value of that stock or bond at the end
of each day. Each holding's investment value is then summed
to arrive at an aggregate investment value for that mutual
fund. That daily aggregate total less any fund liabilities (i.e.
distributions to investors, other) is then divided by the total
number of outstanding shares in that particular mutual fund
to arrive at the daily **Net Asset Value (NAV)**.

The majority of individuals who invest in mutual funds
do so through tax-deferred savings accounts (401K, 403B
or IRA) or other vehicles in which the individual contributes a set amount on a bi-weekly / monthly basis, regardless
of price. This is referred to as **dollar cost averaging**. For
example, if you contribute $1,000 per month to a specific
mutual fund within your 401K account and the price (NAV)

of the mutual fund is $40 in June, you will have purchased twenty-five shares. If the NAV rises to $50 in July, you will only purchase twenty shares, but your June investment will have appreciated by $250. By using this approach, an individual will take the emotion of the daily stock market fluctuations out of play, and over the long run (at least several years) will amass a large number of shares at the same time that the price of a given mutual fund experiences (if history is any guide) an upward trend. This is not to say that every mutual fund returns positive gains for investors. As with any investment, some do better than others, and some mutual funds will post negative returns over time even if the overall market indices increase during that same time.

ETFs

Exchange Trade Funds or ETFs closely mirror the behavior of mutual funds and stocks, by adopting characteristics of both. Like a mutual fund, ETFs contain a basket of stocks and usually track a recognized index such as the Standard & Poors (S&P) 500[52], or a specific sector of the market, such as investments in a particular country (i.e., Germany), region (i.e. Latin America) or industry (i.e. Pharmaceuticals / Biotech). This means that the performance of the ETF will mirror the performance of the particular index it tracks. Unlike a mutual fund, the ETF does not wait until the end of the day to be priced to arrive at a NAV. In this manner it closely resembles a stock where an investor can buy or sell ETFs during the trading day without waiting for the closing day's price to cash out or buy in to a particular mutual fund. The purpose of these products is to allow investors to enjoy

---

52   http://www.investopedia.com/terms/e/etf.asp

the risk diversification of a mutual fund while having the flexibility of buying and selling stocks or bonds.

Bonds

This is another key investment choice for investors, also referred to as a fixed-income instrument because of its nature to remit fixed, periodic interest payments to bondholders (investors). Bondholders purchase the issuer's debt under a contractual agreement that will allow the borrower (bond issuer) to use the bond proceeds for pre-determined purposes in exchange for periodic interest payments and the full reimbursement of the initial principal the lender (bond investor) invested at the time of bond maturity (end of its useful life). Similar to stocks, bonds are used by the issuers (U.S. government, municipalities, and corporations) as a method to finance their respective operations. Unlike stocks, bond prices fluctuate by moving up or down inversely to the direction of interest rates in the marketplace. In a period of rising interest rates, bond prices tend to fall, making them cheaper to purchase. Think of it in the following terms: **If interest rates are rising in the general economy, newly issued bonds (either corporate or government) will offer higher periodic interest payments or yields to consumers in order to keep pace with current economic conditions. When this occurs, existing bonds offering lower interest payments are no longer competitive. Therefore, the price of those existing bonds will fall because the public is not interested in buying them since they can get a better deal elsewhere, and their price to the consumer will fall accordingly.** The process works conversely in the same fashion. A bond has several key features that are necessary for an investor to understand prior to committing funds in this direction.[53] They represent some but not all bond characteristics.

- Maturity: Bonds come with a fixed life, typically ranging anywhere from three months to thirty years. At the end of its life, the bond is said to "**mature**".

- Return of Principal: You get back the entire amount you put in. In essence, **if the bondholder owns the bond until the end of its given life** (maturity), the investor obtains a return of all principal committed (assuming the borrower does not default).

- Callablility: A feature allowing the issuer to redeem the bonds prior to their maturity date. This tends to happen in periods of falling interest rates as bond issuers want to **call back** the bonds and reissue them with lower periodic interest rate obligations (companies tend to do this, not the government). This bond repurchase rewards investors since the amount of money received by the investor consists of the face value of the bond, along with a call premium or a bonus based on the early recall of the bond.

- Face Value: Bonds are normally issued at **par or face value**; for example, $1000. This is a stated amount, which is the basis for the calculation of the semi-annual coupon or interest payment. If the annual coupon rate attached to a $1,000 bond is 6%, you would typically receive $30 every six months until you either sell the bond or it reaches its maturity.

---

53   https://www.key.com/html/bond-investing-benefits.html

- Yield to Maturity: This is the annual compounded rate of return paid out over a bond's life, including price gain/loss and interest earned. This is the **expected annual return or yield a customer could expect to earn on the investment over the life of the bill or bond**. In essence, it provides investors with an idea of the total return they are being promised over the life of the bond.
- Premiums and Discounts: Bonds are sometimes issued by companies at prices below or above face value. If interest rates are rising, which means the bond price is falling, investors will want to be rewarded with a semi-annual interest rate obligation (coupon) that mitigates or offsets the falling bond price, which could result in a net loss for the investor. The company might then issue that bond at a discount to the face value to compensate for higher interest rates available in the marketplace via competing bond issues.

Similar to stocks, investors typically earn a return from their bond holdings in two different manners: price appreciation, and interest (coupon) payments. Even though the investment instrument is as different from common stock as night is from day, the concept of "Buy low, sell high!" still applies. Recall from the **face value** definition that bonds are often issued at par value (i.e., $1,000 Par Value bond sold to an investor for $1,000 is sold at "face value"). If held for the entire life of the bond, the investor would receive all of the semi-annual or periodic coupon payments in addition to the return of principal at the end of the bond's maturity life.

If interest rates fall during the holding period or prior to the bond's maturity, the price of the bond will rise given the reciprocal relationship between bond prices and market interest rates. The investor could earn additional returns by selling the actual bond in the open market, rather than waiting until the bond matures, since it would be worth more money than the face value he paid for it. He would, however, give up the right to any future interest (coupon) payments, but he would have sold the bond for more than he paid for it, netting a capital gain (taxable event) on the transaction.

As in the case of stocks, real estate, precious metals, or any other investment, the investor should gauge his risk/reward tolerance prior to entering into that investment. If the investor has a low tolerance for risk capital, meaning he is not willing to risk much of his disposable income, a bond trading strategy would not fit his investment profile. Instead, bonds would be a great source of income in the sense that they would either be guaranteed (U.S. Treasury bill or bond) or reasonably assured (corporate bonds) a semi-annual interest rate (coupon) payment.

It is important to note that the most common types of bonds to invest in are either U.S. Treasury bills and bonds or corporate bonds. As to the debt's nomenclature, please note that a U.S. Treasury **bill** is a fixed income instrument with a maturity life less than or equal to one year. A U.S. Treasury **note** consists of a fixed income instrument with a life between one and ten years, and a U.S. Treasury **bond** denotes a maturity life between ten and thirty years. Any U.S. Treasury fixed income instrument is backed by the "full faith and credit" of the U.S. government. This means that the payments are **guaranteed** by the U.S. government and will not default under any circumstances. The flip side is that because these investment vehicles are guaranteed and they offer virtually no risk, they also offer very little reward compared to stocks, for instance as long as the instrument is held to maturity.

The price of the Treasury instrument is, however, subject to interest rate movements in the marketplace, and a lot of money can be made or lost depending on the movement of those interest rates. Since the semi-annual interest (coupon) payment is not subject to default, the interest payment to the investor will be less than the interest payment on a corporate bond, which carries a higher degree of risk, requiring additional interest to entice the investor to undertake the risk premium inherent in the corporate bond that offers no guarantee of payment.

Prior to discussing corporate bonds, I'd like to mention another type of government instrument that is very popular with individual investors. Municipal bonds are very similar to U.S. government bonds except that they are issued by municipalities (cities or towns), in order to finance community projects such as building stadiums, community centers, local government offices, etc. These instruments act very much the same way a government bond does except that their periodic interest payments are tax free to investors at the federal level and typically at the state income tax level if you live in the state of issue[54]. Because they are characterized by this addi-

---

54   http://content.municipalbonds.com/2009/01/20/tax-exemption-
the-key-benefit-of-municipal-bonds/

tional benefit, they will typically offer a lower rate of interest to the consumer than a taxable instrument, but they will not result in taxable income. Please note that municipal bonds would still be subject to capital gains taxes similar to a taxable bond issue, if the total sale exceeds the cost of the issue.

Corporate bonds are structured in the same fashion as government fixed income except that there is no guarantee of semi-annual or periodic payments to the bondholders, and they typically offer higher returns or yields, due to the added default risk for these instruments vis a vis US Treasury securities, which are backed by the "full faith and credit" of the U.S. Government, which virtually eliminate default risk. In addition to the general movement in market interest rates, corporate bond prices are directly affected by the company's performance. For example, if interest rates are generally stable, meaning there is no significant fluctuation in the level of consumer and producer prices in the economy, a company's bond price could still move up or down sharply depending on internal factors. If the market perceives that a firm is having difficulty in meeting its cash obligations to its debtors, or if sales are dipping resulting in decreased levels of net income and cash flow to the company, the price of the corporate bonds may still dip significantly. This would force the company to issue bonds promising higher interest rate yields (expected returns) to its bondholders in order to continue attracting customers.

Real Estate

For the average American, the primary residence will comprise the largest portion of their asset base and, in turn, net worth. Remember the formula for net worth:

Assets – Liabilities = Net Worth

Since most Americans are saddled with mortgages (mortgage = debt owed to the bank on the property), the total fair market value of the property, less the balance owed on the mortgage constitutes the homeowner's net worth in the house. That resulting balance is then added to all of the other assets in the consumer's portfolio, which will include stocks, bonds, other real estate holdings, precious metals, valuables, etc. to arrive at one's total asset base. All other liabilities, which will include consumer or credit card debt balances, student loans, automobile loans, and all other forms of debt, are subtracted from one's total asset base resulting in a consumer's net worth or net loss position.

In addition to personal property, many Americans choose to invest disposable income by purchasing investment property. Although it usually refers to a second home, it can also be office property, timeshares for vacation purposes, etc... Like stocks and bonds, there are two principal ways of increasing one's net worth from investment properties: rental income and price appreciation. When purchasing a second home, the buyer will usually take on a new mortgage since the odds of paying for a new home in cash are fairly small. Many owners will then rent the property to tenants in the hope that the tenant's rental payments will be sufficient to pay down the mortgage, property taxes, and insurance costs. Any money remaining after the monthly bills have been paid on the new property will serve to increase the owner's cash flow position.

As is the case with a primary residence, home values for investment properties are expected to appreciate over a protracted period of time. Therefore, if a rental property is held for a long enough period of time, the buyer will hopefully be able to sell the property for a greater amount than was paid for it. Although home prices generally increase in value over time, this is not a guarantee, so timing is critical because many times property values will go down for certain stretches of time even though, for the long run, the trend is generally upward. Caution: investment properties carry a higher mortgage interest rate then primary residence mortgages, due to the perceived risk by the lender that should the borrower fall on hard times, he would likely do what he can to pay the mortgage on the primary residence before worrying about payments on the rental property.

Precious Metals

Prior to the 1970s, all currency in the United States was backed by gold, primarily to ensure that the currency retained its value in the marketplace. During the Nixon administration, the government was continually forced to convert dollars to gold at the price of $35 an ounce, a price which had been in effect since the Roosevelt administration, more than three decades prior. As inflationary pressures began taking hold in the economy, Nixon found this situation to be untenable and took the U.S. off the gold standard, essentially removing this price control from the economy (before re-imposing price controls at a later date) which allowed both the currency and the price of gold to float freely.[55] Currency

---

55   http://www.pbs.org/wgbh/commandingheights/shared/minitext/ ess_nixongold.html

without any backing is referred to as **fiat currency**. Inflation is defined as an increase in the amount of money or credit available in relation to the amount of goods or services available, which causes an increase in the general price level of goods and services. Inflation reduces the purchasing power of a dollar, making it worth less.[56] By the time the 1970s were over, the price of gold had risen to almost $700 an ounce[57] (Today, it is more than double that level sitting at approximately $1,800 an ounce). As the value of the U.S. dollar weakened over the course of the '70s, many investors chose to invest in gold, silver, and platinum as well as other commodities such as oil, grains, and pork-bellies. The reason was two-fold: Americans saw a huge opportunity for price appreciation, but they also wanted to protect their net worth against inflation rates, which reached as high as 14 percent in 1980.[58] Gold has often been considered a wonderful hedge against inflation. Unlike stocks and bonds, investing in precious metals does not offer the opportunity to obtain periodic payments such as interest payments (coupon interest), dividends or rental income. However, during periods of great volatility in the stock and bond markets, investors in precious metals have always benefited by preserving part of their total asset base.

Savings Plans and CDs

Some investors do not want to assume any level of risk. Individuals who have amassed large quantities of money

---

56   http://www.investordictionary.com/definition/inflation.aspx

57   http://www.kitco.com/scripts/hist_charts/yearly_graphs.cgi

58   http://inflationdata.com/Inflation/Inflation_Rate/
       HistoricalInflation.aspx?dsInflation_current

during their lives may not have much of a desire in growing their asset base as they enter into their golden years, but would rather preserve what they have. "Don't lose the principal" is one of the oldest axioms of wealthy families. In addition, many individuals and couples might not have any tolerance for risk and would rather sacrifice greater reward for the comfort of eliminating virtually all investment risk. Bank savings accounts and certificates of deposit (CDs) are perfect investment vehicles for these individuals. These vehicles return money to investors by paying periodic interest on top of the principal deposited. Savings accounts allow the individual to pull their money out at any time without any penalty. For a slightly higher interest rate return, certificates of deposit provide a periodic interest rate payment (slightly higher than savings accounts) as long as the investor deposits money with that financial institution for a pre-determined period of time, normally three months, six months, or one year. Unlike savings accounts, CDs may impose a penalty upon premature withdrawal of the funds.

The following table provides a glimpse into annual rates of return (which include an inflation premium) provided by different investment vehicles. It is an accepted fact that over time, stocks (equities) provide the greatest annual rates of return. This is not to recommend stocks at the exclusion of any other investment vehicles. In fact, a balanced portfolio or asset composition should comprise a mixture of stocks, bonds, real estate and possibly commodities, and savings accounts in order to spread as much of the risk inherent in each of those instruments as possible. Simply said, investors should not put all their eggs in one basket.

| Historical Annual Returns 1926-2009 ||
Asset Class	Return (% / yr)
Stocks (Small Company)	11.2%
Stocks (Large Company)	9.8%
Real Estate*	5.9%
US Treasury Bonds (30 yr)	5.5%
Gold	5.1%
Cash (Money Market)	3.7%
Inflation	3.0%

* Annual return since 1963   [59]

Investment Vehicles

The first part of this chapter has been dedicated to explaining the most common investment types. In this section, we will focus on the different ways in which investors can buy and sell these different types of investment options. I have suggested that it would behoove individuals to follow a certain order in the development of their personal finances in order to prevent "falling BEHIND the 8 ball." First a Budget should be created that would help determine the amount of disposable income available to a household. Individuals and couples would then be able to prioritize how to pay down and consolidate their debts as well as to plan for future obligations, i.e. a child's education or the purchase of

---

59   www.am-a.com/protected/education/ed_products/workbook/
      hist_performance.htm

a new car. A key underlying assumption at this stage is that the individual is significantly contributing to a tax deferred savings account (TDS), such as a 401K, 403B or IRA plan for nest egg building purposes. Once a plan is in place to Eliminate all debts, an individual should focus on Home ownership. Subsequent to purchasing a primary residence, which will usually become the household's greatest asset, I suggest that individuals begin to Invest certain amounts of disposable income in growth instruments such as stocks, bonds, real estate, precious metals, and savings plans.

401k and 403b Plans

The primary purpose of these investment vehicles is to fund a household's retirement. Saving for your retirement does not have to present difficulties as long as you are aware of your options. These two plans are very similar with one critical distinction being that for-profit companies use 401k plans and non-profit companies use 403b plans. An employee contributes a pre-determined percentage (of his own choosing) from every paycheck to these vehicles with pre-tax dollars. This means that the account can appreciate and ongoing contributions can continue being made to the account **without being taxed** until the individual retires or reaches seventy and one-half. The key is that these contributions are not included in one's reported income, which is subject to taxation. In essence, you receive an immediate tax deduction for your contribution.

Many employers offer an automatic payroll deduction, so there isn't any extra effort involved for the investor. Matching contribution incentives are frequently offered by employers that offer 401k and 403b plans, mostly for employee retention purposes. For instance, some employers match every dollar contribution by the investor with "X" cents on the dollar; meaning, if you contribute 8% of your monthly salary to your retirement plan, the employer might match every percentage up to 3% or 4% on a 1:1 ratio, meaning that you might actually be saving 11% - 12% of your salary each month. Over the course of a few decades this can result in many hundreds of thousands of dollars in retirement savings generated by the thrifty employee. Of course, with any government sponsored legislation such as tax deferred savings plans, there are rules and regulations. The key one being that you are limited in your annual contributions to a percentage of your income not to exceed $16,500 (2011 dollars).

So what happens if you leave your company? You have a few options: leave the monies in place; **roll them over** into another tax-deferred retirement account such as an **IRA** or another company's 401k or 403b plan; or withdraw some or all of the savings from the tax deferred vehicle. However, if you choose to withdraw some or all of your tax-deferred savings, an early withdrawal penalty will apply in almost all situations, should the withdrawal occur before you are fifty-nine and one-half years of age. This penalty equates to 10 percent of the amount withdrawn plus any taxes owed on the profits earned from contributions to the plan.

If at all possible, avoid withdrawing any funds before age fifty-nine and one-half. That doesn't mean however, that you have to start spending those savings immediately thereafter. Mandatory withdrawal occurs when the investor turns seventy and one-half years of age, forcing the individual to begin making **minimum distribution** taxable withdrawals on those monies accumulated over many years. Minimum distribution payments are amounts calculated according to specific federal tax rules, requiring investors to begin paying taxes on savings that have been compounding for years under the protection of their company's 401k or 403b plan. Monies saved under the protection of regular IRA plans are also subject to this minimum distribution rule.

Your 401k or 403b portfolio should be chosen carefully, weighing age and risk factors. First and foremost, the employee should contribute as much as possible up to the maximum amount allowed by law. This is referred to as **maxing out your account.** Remember that the contribution is tax-deferred, so if you do not take advantage of the total allowable contribution, you are in essence leaving free money on the table. This results in lost investment potential as these are un-invested dollars not being allowed to compound in a tax-deferred manner.

Most tax-deferred plans offer the employee the opportunity to invest in mutual funds and/or cash. The respective funds are normally broken down into stock based or bond based, or hybrid funds, which combine both stocks and bonds and offer the employee domestic versus international investment options. Stocks historically have offered the greatest annual rates of return of any investment option; however, those returns are accompanied by slightly higher degrees of risk than bonds typically have. As previously mentioned in the mutual fund section of this chapter, 401k plans, 403b plans, or IRAs offer you the ability to **dollar cost average** your investments. In this way, constant stock and bond market fluctuations are in essence ignored because whether the stock market goes up or down within a certain period of time, you are investing the same total dollar amount each month. If the particular mutual fund prices in your plan drop in one month it means that your monthly contribution will buy a greater number of shares and vice-versa. With dollar cost averaging, you should expect your investments to appreciate over time if history is any indicator. However, there are no guarantees and all investors should be aware of their risk tolerance prior to investing monies in any of these instruments.

I would suggest that the younger the employee is, the greater the percentage of higher growth investment vehicles be included in the portfolio. Therefore, a 35 year-old's portfolio would probably consist of a greater percentage of stocks or stock mutual funds than bonds or bond mutual funds, given that the relative youth of the investor will allow for a greater degree of risk to be undertaken since **growth** and not **preservation of capital** is the main objective at this stage. However, if you are not comfortable with that level of risk, then simply choose fewer stocks or stock mutual funds. Do remember this: Over the last century, the stock market has returned an average of approximately 9% per annum; including dividend payments (this includes all wars and the Great Depression). Choose wisely and consider how much risk you are willing to take. Most of all, you need to be comfortable with your choices. If you need further assistance in choosing your investment options, there are investment resources such as **Morningstar**, which provides an analysis of hundreds of different mutual funds.[60]

One by product of 401k plans that has come on the scene in recent years is the **Solo 401k**[61]. This tax deferred savings plan applies to self employed individuals who run a "one person" shop. The plan offers significant advantages to many other retirement plans currently available in the marketplace, the largest being large deductibles and large annual contributions. First, you can contribute up to 100% of the first $16,500 of your 2010 compensation or self-employment income ($22,000 if you'll be 50 or older at year-end). And there's more: You can contribute and deduct an additional amount of up to 25% of your compensation income, or 20% of your self-employment income. This second part of your annual contribution is similar to what you can do with a traditional small-business retirement plan. What is the impact to me? For example, if your annual income is $80,000, you can legally contribute up to $32,500 to your solo 401K account. In traditional self directed IRA accounts the maximum contribution would be 25% of the annual salary or $20,000. The total cap for solo 401K contributions in 2010 is $49,000 or $54,500 if you are over 50 years of age by 12/31/10.

IRA Accounts

The creation of savings plans are not a right of work nor are employers required to provide them. There are

---

60   http://www.morningstar.com/#A1
61   http://online.wsj.com/article/SB10001424052748704039704574
      616230013475734.html

millions of people who either work for themselves or work in small companies that don't offer employee tax-deferred savings plans. IRA accounts are a terrific alternative for these individuals. They have the same general character-istics of 401k and 403b plans but offer restricted tax-deferral amounts. There are two types of IRA plans: regular (also referred to as traditional), and Roth IRAs. Since both offer tax deductible characteristics, contribution amounts are limited, and tax deductibility depends on the level of income of the investor. For 2010, you are allowed a tax deductible contribution of up to $5,000 to your IRA, up to the age of 49. Workers 50 years of age and older may deduct contributions up to $6,000. If you have more than one account, you may contribute to all of them, as long as the total contributed is not greater than the yearly limit per account. Please note that you may contribute more than these amounts; however, the excess over the limits set below will not be tax deductible.

Traditional & Roth IRA Contribution Limits

Year	Contribution Limits	Catch-Up Provision Limit
2010	$ 5,000	$ 6,000
2011	$ 5,000	$ 6,000
2012	Indexed to Inflation	Indexed to Inflation
2013	Indexed to Inflation	Indexed to Inflation

http://beginnersinvest.about.com/cs/iras/a/iracontribution.htm

Traditional IRAs

Similar to 401k and 403b plans, the earnings on a Traditional IRA grow tax-deferred, which means you do not owe income taxes until you begin to take distributions from the account. In addition, you can begin to take penalty-free distributions from a Traditional IRA in the year after you reach age fifty-nine and one-half. In most cases, you must pay an early withdrawal penalty if you take a distribution sooner. Traditional IRAs are also similar to 401K and 403b plans in that you are required to take distributions when you reach age seventy and one-half, subject to **required minimum distribution (RMD)** rules.

- If you earn too much income, or already participate in a 401k or similar retirement plan, your tax-deductible contributions to a regular IRA are gradually phased out. This means that some of your contributions to a regular IRA cannot be deducted from your income. The contributions that are not tax-deductible are called **non-deductible contributions**. Following are the income limits at which your tax-deductible contributions phase out:
- **Single filers that participate in a 401k or 403b plan:** If your modified adjusted gross income (MAGI) is more than $56,000 and less than $66,000 in 2011, some of your contribution is non-deductible. Above $66,000 of income, your entire contribution is non-deductible (tax terms will be discussed in the tax section at the end of the handbook).

Married persons filing a joint return, if you, but not your spouse, participate in a 401k or 403b plan: If modified adjusted gross income is more than $90,000 and less than $109,000 in 2011, some of your contribution is non-deductible. Above $109,000 your entire contribution is non-deductible. Married persons with neither spouse contributing to a 401k / 403b plan have no income limits.

2011 Traditional IRA Deduction Limits
If Covered by a Retirement Plan at Work

Filing Status	Full Deduction	Phase-Out	No Deduction
Single	< $56,000	$56,000 - $66,000	> $66,000
Married Filing Joint	< $90,000	$90,000 - $109,000	> $109,000

http://www.money-zine.com/Financial-Planning/Retirement/IRA-Contribution-Limits/

Roth IRAs

Individuals can contribute up to $5,000 to a Roth IRA for 2011. The same catch-up provision allows persons age fifty or older to contribute up to $6,000 to a Roth IRA or combination of accounts. A big difference in regular IRAs and Roth IRAs is that contributions to Roth IRAs are **NOT tax-deductible**. Instead, the contributions are made after paying income taxes. This disadvantage would seem to favor Traditional IRAs. However, if you keep a Roth IRA for at least five years and are age fifty-nine and one-half, become disabled, die, or incur expenses related to a first-time home purchase, the amount is exempt from income tax and IRS penalties. **Think of this. Under these criteria, all earnings from a Roth IRA are TAX FREE upon withdrawal. In** addition, you can earn significantly more salary under Roth IRA rules and still have the ability to contribute to your plan.

One of the nice features of the Roth IRA is that anyone - at any age - can contribute to a Roth as long as they have some form of compensation and a non-working spouse. Income limit rules apply as follows:

- Single filers with modified adjusted gross income up to $107,000 can make a full contribution. If your adjusted gross income is in excess of $122,000, then you cannot make a contribution to a Roth IRA.
- Joint filers with modified adjusted gross income up to $169,000 can make a full contribution. If your adjusted gross income is in excess of $179,000, then you cannot make a contribution to a Roth IRA.

2011 Roth IRA Deduction Limits

Filing Status	Full Deduction	Phase-Out
Single	<$107,000	$107,000 - $122,000
Married Filing Joint	<$169,000	$169,000 - $179,000

http://www.money-zine.com/Financial-Planning/Retirement/IRA-Cont

Finally, Roth IRAs do not have required minimum distributions, which give you more flexibility in planning your estate. If you wish, you can leave the entire amount of a Roth IRA to your beneficiaries.[62]

---

62   http://www.rothira.com/

SEP Accounts
- SEP accounts are simplified employee pension (SEP) accounts. It is another type of IRA account and is targeted at very small businesses, independent contractors, and sole proprietorships. A SEP plan allows an employer to make contributions toward employees' retirement, and, if self-employed, his or her own retirement, without becoming involved in more complex retirement plans. A self-employed individual is an employee for SEP purposes. He or she is also the employer. Even if the self-employed individual is the only qualifying employee, he or she can have a SEP-IRA. A qualifying employee meets the following conditions[63]:
- At least twenty-one years of age
- Worked for employer for at least three of the five years immediately preceding the tax year
- Has received from the employer at least $550 in compensation in the tax year

Note: Employers can establish less restrictive participation requirements for their employees than those listed, but not more restrictive ones.

SEP Advantages
- Contributions to a SEP are tax deductible and your business pays no taxes on the earnings on the investments.

---

[63] http://www.dol.gov/ebsa/publications/SEPPlans.html

- You are not locked into making contributions every year. In fact, you decide each year whether, and how much, to contribute to your employees' SEP-IRAs.
- Generally, you do not have to file any documents with the government.
- Sole proprietors, partnerships, and corporations, including S corporations, can set up SEPs.
- Administrative costs are low.

Note: SEP accounts allow for maximum annual contributions equal to 25% of your annual salary, not to exceed a maximum amount of $49,000 in contributions. For an annual salary of $80,000, the maximum legal contribution to this tax-deferred account would be $16,000.

Brokerage Accounts

In order to achieve financial freedom, you must first have your priorities straight. As mentioned previously, it makes little sense to invest in **taxable** stocks and bonds that are not part of a pre-determined retirement plan (i.e.; a Roth IRA) which will yield uncertain returns when carrying credit card balances with annual interest rates in the mid to high teens or worse. All of the previous investment vehicles with the exception of the Roth IRA have been **tax-deferred**. Individuals should take full advantage of these tax-deferred savings and investment plans regardless of whether they still have debt, rent an apartment, or have yet to prepare a personal financial plan. It is the **taxable** investment accounts I would recommend avoiding until a plan is in place to deal with consumer and other debt obligations and the purchase of a primary residence.

The term brokerage is derived from broker. A broker or stockbroker is the individual entrusted to buy and sell stock for the investor at a particular price. This person may also be licensed to buy and sell bonds, real estate, commodities, and other types of investment instruments. This individual will normally receive a commission or payment based on the difference between the purchase and the selling price, also known as **the spread**. Other investment companies will charge the customer a percentage of all assets invested with that company which is referred to as a **fee for service**.

Taxable brokerage accounts are regular investment accounts, primarily directed at stocks and bonds, which are subject to different types of taxes depending on whether a profit is generated through the sale of shares of common stock or bonds, or whether regular, periodic dividend or interest payments are received. Capital gains taxes are due when a sale of stock or bonds results in a net gain for the investor. Dividend and bond interest (coupon payments) received is considered to be part of one's regular income generation and thus subject to ordinary income taxes based on the individual's stated tax bracket.

Section 529 Savings Plans

There is another wonderful tax-deferred savings vehicle available to consumers. However, as with taxable investment or brokerage accounts, I would encourage parents to contribute to the following investment vehicles at such time as they have a clear household budget defined, have made substantial progress in eliminating their high interest debt, and have begun the process of purchasing a home.

There are several large unknowns in any household budget, and most families actually do not even plan for some of the more costly expenditures such as: a) education for children and b) nursing/long-term care. The latter will be discussed in the next chapter. Today, families who would like to pay for their children's college education are faced with spiraling, out-of-control costs for college, in some cases exceeding $50,000 per year per child depending on the school. College costs typically rise at a rate faster than inflation, so use that as a guide when estimating your college tuition needs.

Many families are only able to pay for a portion of their child's college education, if any at all, resulting in situations where children may need to borrow large amounts of money for student loans. Let me first state that there is nothing wrong with college-bound students paying for **part** of their education. In fact, it is often their first encounter with true responsibility and it is a great life lesson in thriftiness. No parent wants to see their son or daughter saddled with tens of thousands of dollars in student loan debt (or worse) before they begin their working careers, but the upside is that it builds character and teaches individuals accountability. There are several ways parents can ease the burden of student loan debt for their kids. One of these is by proper planning early in their children's lives by employing such investment tools as tax-deferred savings plans, which we will discuss below.

Congress authorized Section 529 Education Savings Plans in 1996. Currently, all 50 states offer at least one version of a 529 plan. These plans were designed to complement the already existing prepaid tuition plans that many states had established. There are two types of 529 plans: **prepaid tuition plans** and **college savings plans**[64]. Prepaid tuition plans allow college savers to purchase "units" or credits at participating universities, locking in tuition prices at today's dollars, guaranteeing that a regular plan of savings will mature to pay college semesters, regardless of the effect of inflation on future college costs. The 529 College Savings Plan establishes an account for the "saver" for the purpose of paying college expenses. The College Savings Plan adds a degree of risk, because the ultimate value depends on the performance of the investments within the plan (much like a 401k plan). But even with that risk, Section 529 Savings Plans have some great advantages over other college savings techniques.

Section 529 Plans are highly flexible. The money in a Section 529 College Savings Plan can be used for educational expenses at any accredited school in any state. In Section 529 Plans, assets can easily be transferred among family beneficiaries. If one child does not use the money for college, the person who contributed to the plan (called the participant) can easily designate another child, a cousin, a niece or nephew, themselves, or an unrelated person. Thus,

---

64   http://www.sec.gov/investor/pubs/intro529.htm

grandparents who set up the plans can switch the money between grandchildren. A participant could set up his own plan and later transfer the assets to his child.

If college savings are in different types of vehicles such as Uniform Gifts to Minors Act (UGMA) accounts, an irrevocable custodial plan, parents may lose control over the money when the child reaches the age of majority (eighteen in certain states). **The parent may have been saving for Princeton, but the child may choose a Porsche.** With a Section 529 Plan, the participant retains control over the assets until the assets are distributed to pay for education.

Section 529 Plans also have estate tax advantages. Although most plans will be started with a small initial investment and regular contributions, the law allows one-time gifts as well. There is currently no contribution limit to Section 529 plans, however, the contribution will be treated as a "gift" subject to gift tax treatment[65]. The contributor can aggregate five years of the allowable $13,000 annual gift tax (see tax section) exclusion to jump-start a Section 529 Investment Plan, with an initial contribution of $65,000. However, this contribution will be made with the knowledge that it was done over a five year period to remain compliant with gift tax limitations. Wealthy grandparents might consider making a large gift to get cash out of their estate, but they will be subject to Federal Gift Tax contribution limits. Even if the donors are somewhat worried about needing the money, or if the recipient is uninterested in

---

65   http://www.ehow.com/about_5381610_plan-contribution-limits. html

college, the donor retains control over the gift. The donor can take back the gift at any time after paying the income tax plus a federally mandated 10% penalty for early withdrawal. This allows a participant to remove the funds from their estate for estate tax purpose but have access to the cash if later needed.

As of January 2006, assets in Section 529 plans are now considered a student asset in formulas used to determine financial aid[66], which means families and students may be declared ineligible for government assistance in education. This mirrors other plans such as assets held in UGMA custodial accounts, where student assets are counted heavily in the financial aid formula.

Many other college savings plans either limit the amount of contributions each year or place restrictions on parental income. With 529 plans the participant does not have to be a parent, grandparent, or even a relative. A participant can make a contribution for any living beneficiary who plans to continue her education. If an adult participant plans to attend law or medical school, he can contribute his own savings to a Section 529 Plan. If he does not use the money, children can. Also, as a child earns money in summer jobs and after school, that money can be deposited to grow tax-free in a Section 529 Plan. Please note the exclusion limits change from one year to the next, so although the amounts may vary by the time you read this, the overall advantage gained by using these plans remains in effect.

66   http://www.sec.gov/investor/pubs/intro529.htm

Parents considering switching from another prepaid tuition plan to a Section 529 Plan must sell the assets in other custodial accounts and pay the taxes, because only cash can be invested in the Section 529 Plan. There will be limits on how the funds can actually be spent. Section 529 Plans require the savings to be spent only on a student's tuition, room and board, fees, books, and supplies. Money taken from a 529 plan and used for other purposes is subject to a 10% penalty.

Looking at this issue from the child's or student's perspective, a 529 Savings Plan means that those monies will be there for educational purposes at such time the desire is there to attend a university or trade school. A graduating high school senior may decide that she wants to travel or work for a couple of years prior to entering college. This savings vehicle offers the individual that flexibility and comfort of knowing that those funds will be there when the time is right. One caveat: these funds **cannot** be used to bolster a student's beer budget ☺.

Education IRAs (aka Coverdell Savings Accounts) are another college savings vehicle and offer annual contributions up to $2,000. Married households earning below $220,000 are eligible to contribute to these accounts ($110,000 for single households). With an Education IRA, the owner can self-direct the investments, similar to other IRAs. Section 529 Plans are limited to mutual fund accounts offered by the plans. Money saved in an Education IRA can be used for private and religious elementary and secondary schools, while

Section 529 assets can only be used to pay for expenses at an approved institution of higher education.[67]

One final method of education financing I would like to mention is the use of **zero coupon bonds.** These are bonds that do not pay interest during the entire life of the bond. Instead, buyers are enticed to purchase these bonds because they are issued at a deep discount from their face value. For example a $10,000 face value, municipal, zero coupon bond might have a purchase price of approximately $6,000. The point is that if the buyer holds the bond for a protracted period of time, say twenty years, at the bond's maturity the bondholder will receive the full face value of $10,000. The downside is that there will be no periodic interest payments received. From an education financing standpoint, this can be thought of as a down payment on the child's future college education costs. Many states will issue a version of these with names such as **Illinois College Savings Bond.**[68]

ASSET ALLOCATION

In this chapter, we have discussed many different types of investments available to consumers, as well as the available vehicles with which to enter into these investments, both from a taxable and tax-deferred perspective. The key remaining question centers around how much to invest in each instrument, or how much money should be allocated to each asset type, given that most households have only so much disposable income available to invest.

---

67 http://www.statefarm.com/learning/life_stages/college_fund/coverdel.asp

68 http://www.state.il.us/budget/bonds.htm

DO NOT PUT ALL YOUR EGGS IN ONE BASKET

Take the Smith family for instance. If they have a significant sum of available income to invest, they would be undertaking an excessive risk if most or the entire amount were to be invested in the same stock, bond, mutual fund or other investment type. It would be prudent to spread the funds throughout several different investments in order to **diversify** (spread) as much of the risk inherent in those investment options as possible.

Any investment decision involves choosing one investment over another, given that most individuals are dealing with limited choices of mutual funds within their tax deferred savings plans. Choosing one investment over another is known as the **opportunity cost** of making that investment, since the Smith's would be unable to own all of the available investment choices. Therefore, they would need to make a decision as to which investments will provide them with the greatest rate of return opportunity. When making this investment decision, they need to assess the level of risk they are willing to undertake in the hopes of growing their funds as much as possible. This is known as the **risk/reward** ratio of the investor. No matter how much or how little risk the Smith's are willing to assume when putting the funds to work, the assets should be allocated in order to diversify away as much risk as possible while trying to generate the greatest potential return.

Please note the only **guaranteed** investment option is a U.S. Treasury security. It is backed by the full faith and credit of the U.S. government which has not defaulted on a loan promise in the entire history of this country. In March of 2011, a U.S. Treasury bond with a 10 year maturity, carried an interest rate of approximately 3.5%. This is the **risk free rate of interest**. Any long term investment opportunities with expected rates of return above 3.5%, by definition, incorporate some level of risk. The greater the expected return, the greater the additional risk the investor is assuming.

HOW SHOULD CONSUMERS DIVERSIFY THEIR RISK?

Investors often make the mistake of thinking that just because they spread the available funds in different investment options that they are diversifying their risk. Not necessarily! Often times, novice investors will choose different mutual funds or other investment choices within their company savings plan, which end up having very **similar investment objectives**. The only result is that the individual ends up with two different investment choices with the same investment types.

In order to properly diversify, you must first assess the level of risk you are willing to undertake. Although everyone's risk tolerance is different, younger people who have relatively small accumulations of assets should be willing to accept higher degrees of risk in their investment options than they would 20-30 years down the road, as their primary goal is the **growth** of their portfolio. Older individuals, who have spent many years building their asset bases, are probably less willing to risk losing what they have worked so hard to build. They will most likely gear their investment selections to stocks, bonds, mutual funds, or real estate investments that are focused on **preserving their capital** base with limited growth rather than risking capital on investment options that offer more aggressive growth opportunities.

Once you arrive at a personal risk profile, you can begin to allocate the investment funding appropriately by breaking down your investment selections in terms of percentages. Following are two schedules reflecting sample asset allocations for a younger and an older investor. As you can see, the older investor might gear the investment choices to alternatives offering a lower risk and a higher opportunity to preserve capital. The younger investor would be expected to gear her investment choices towards alternatives offering higher growth opportunities. While younger investors would be prudent in accepting a higher level of risk, I would suggest that a significant portion of their available investment funds be geared towards proven investments; that is, more mature companies, and a smaller portion of available investment funds be targeted towards more aggressive, risk-laden investments rather than the other way around. If most of your available investment funds are targeted at high risk/high reward stocks, bonds or mutual funds, you may be crossing the line from prudent investing to aggressive investing or speculation.

Growth Oriented Portfolio - Younger Investor

Investment Goal	Definition	% Allocation
Growth Only	Smaller Companies w/ High Growth Potential / No Dividends	40%
Growth & Income	Fully Mature Companies w/ Dividends + Smaller Companies w/ High Growth Potential / No Dividends	30%
Income Only	High Dividend Payments / Bonds	20%
Cash	Money Market Accounts	10%

Income Oriented Portfolio - Older Investor

Investment Goal	Definition	% Allocation
Growth Only	Smaller Companies w/ High Growth Potential / No Dividends	10%
Growth & Income	Fully Mature Companies w/ Dividends + Smaller Companies w/ High Growth Potential / No Dividends	30%
Income Only	High Dividend Payments / Bonds	30%
Cash	Money Market Accounts	30%

Obviously these examples are by no means the rule. Every investor has different levels of risk that they are willing to assume in their portfolios. Some older individuals are much more comfortable with higher risk levels while some younger investors are virtually risk intolerant. The risk/reward ratio is what tends to be true, but the percentages and the investment types will vary widely for all investors.

This is not an advanced finance book, so concepts are intentionally kept at a higher level than some other textbooks might with respect to similar issues. However, with respect to asset allocation principles, the concept of **correlation** needs to be addressed. When two investments are **positively correlated**, their share prices are expected to move in a similar pattern because their performance will be impacted by similar industry / economic forces. For instance, low interest rates tend to help most banking stocks, since it is assumed their costs will decrease and they will be able to at least maintain loan rates to borrowers at current levels, helping them to increase profits.

When two investments are **negatively correlated**, their share prices might move in different directions a high percentage of the time, because similar economic forces might impact them differently. For example, a long protracted winter season might negatively impact a company that sells lawn mowers while a company selling skis and winter apparel might benefit significantly for the same reasons.

I raise this issue, because often times, investors believe (somewhat erroneously) that they can mitigate risk in their investments by purchasing a risky asset and then purchasing a non-risky asset. While that **may** reduce some of their risk exposure, they may actually be better off purchasing stocks with relatively high expected rates of return that carry above market risk levels, which are more negatively correlated, meaning that expected investment returns should achieve somewhat opposite results. This may seem counterintuitive, but significant research exists that validates this hypothesis.[69]

SHOULD I BUY AND SELL INDIVIDUAL STOCKS?

Many individuals shy away from purchasing individual common stock for fear they will lose significant amounts of

---

69   http://en.wikipedia.org/wiki/Modern_portfolio_theory

money, opting instead to purchase mutual funds which are managed by "professionals" who are supposed to invest client funds in such a way that mitigates much of the risk of investing. Losing money is certainly a possibility, particularly if you do not know what you are doing (even if you do, there is no guarantee of investment profits). However, by simply learning a few key metrics, an individual investor can go a long way towards de-mystifying investments in individual companies.

Before we begin, two critical factors need to be addressed. First, it is important to remember that a company's common stock price is nothing more than a **claim** on future earnings by the investment community. It is expected profits (earnings), and the ability to generate future cash flows that entice investors to purchase the stock of a particular company. If the company is successful at growing its future earnings and cash flows, then it will continue to expand. Investors will not purchase stock if they think the company will decrease its future earnings for each share sold to the public. For instance, you don't want to purchase shares in a company that produces the best video cassette recorders. DVDs made them obsolete.

Second, many in the investment community believe that markets are **efficient**; that is, that all information available to the public at large is currently priced into the stock price of a particular firm. Although I may be in the minority, I do NOT subscribe to this hypothesis. I believe that if an investor does his homework, then he may be able to consistently select stocks that are undervalued;

meaning, that the value of the company is greater than the value the market is placing on that firm at that particular time.

As with anything else, once you learn the underlying fundamentals of any new discipline, you will go a long way towards understanding the concepts. Investing in individual companies without the advisory services of a professional, should be undertaken only after you have first assessed your individual risk tolerance and determined that this path makes sense for you and your household. Once you have decided to go down this path, you should make the effort to learn the fundamentals of corporate financial statements. It is the information gleaned from these statements that will allow you to employ the necessary knowledge that will drive successful investing. There are three key corporate financial statements: a) the Income Statement b) the Balance Sheet and c) the Statement of Cash Flows. In this book, we will concentrate on the first two.

INCOME STATEMENT

Much like your personal budget, the income statement is a statement of financial performance, usually over a three month period. It answers the questions, "How did company XYZ perform over a specific period of time?" It does this by reconciling total sales (revenues) against total expenses. The remaining value is the company's net income or earnings over that period of time. In essence, a company tabulates total sales and subtracts all related costs incurred in arriving at those sales. Below is a sample income statement from Amgen Corporation:

Income Statement - AMGEN Corporation ($K)	12/31/2010	12/31/2009	12/31/2008
Revenue	$ 15,053,000	$ 14,642,000	$ 15,003,000
Cost of Revenue	2,220,000	$ 2,091,000	$ 2,296,000
Gross Profit / (Loss)	$ 12,833,000	$ 12,551,000	$ 12,707,000
Operating Expenses			
Researcg & Development	2,894,000	2,864,000	3,030,000
Selling, General & Administrative	4,100,000	3,887,000	4,169,000
Other	294,000	294,000	294,000
Operating Income / (Loss)	$ 5,545,000	$ 5,506,000	$ 5,214,000
Other Income	376,000	276,000	352,000
Earnings Before Interest & Taxes	5,921,000	5,782,000	5,566,000
Interest Expense	604,000	578,000	316,000
Income Before Tax	5,317,000	5,204,000	5,250,000
Income Tax Expencse	690,000	599,000	1,054,000
Net Income	$ 4,627,000	$ 4,605,000	$ 4,196,000
Outstanding Shares (K)	932,450		

70

Notice that there is a distinct format for income statements. First, total revenues are calculated by adding up all sales for that year. Total sales will be the product of all unit sales * selling prices for the respective products. Cost of Goods Sold or **direct costs** will be subtracted from sales to arrive at a **gross profit**. Direct costs comprise all costs directly identified to the manufacture of the product that is sold. This includes labor of individuals producing the product, or direct labor; it also includes raw materials purchased to produce the product; finally the factory space, electricity usage and other ancillary costs (known as factory overhead) identifiable in building the product would also be included in direct costs.

Once the direct costs are identified, you will then need to subtract all **indirect** expenses associated with the sale of that product from the gross profit. Indirect costs are costs

70   http://finance.yahoo.com/q/is?s=AMGN+Income+Statement&annual

not directly associated with the manufacture of the product, but instead comprise the "infrastructure" of the company. For instance, these include paying for the marketing department and sales team; the executive management and human resources departments; the accounting and finance organizations, as well as the legal department and research and development efforts aimed at the introduction of future products and services for the company. Depreciation and amortization costs are also deducted at this point if applicable. These are costs aimed at periodically accounting for the cost of large capital investments in building and equipment. The idea is to recognize these costs periodically rather than all at once, due to their significant size, and the damaging impact that could result to a company's bottom line. Once all of these costs are identified and subtracted from gross profit, a company is left with its operating profit.

Operating profit is important because it reflects the income from continuing operations. It is an excellent way of evaluating the performance of the company from quarter to quarter, or from year to year or against industry peers, **because all costs incurred to this point are the types of costs that are expected to recur in the future**. After this metric has been reached, two key components are left for the company to deduct in order to arrive at the final net income. These are interest and taxes. Interest reflects the company's periodic obligations on any loans (debt) borrowed from financial institutions. The more the company borrows to finance its expansion, the higher the interest costs are expected to be. Once these costs are accounted for, the last key remaining income statement component are the taxes the company owes to the federal government. This percentage typically ranges between 35% and 40% of all income before taxes and is currently the second highest corporate tax rate in the industrialized world, right behind Japan!

BALANCE SHEET

Much like the statement of personal net worth, companies use their balance sheets to obtain a snapshot at any point in time of their net worth, by tabulating all of their assets (items owned) and liabilities (debts). The difference between the two results in the company's net worth or capital position. Below is an example of a corporate balance sheet.

Balance Sheet - AMGEN Corporation ($K)	12/31/2010	12/31/2009	12/31/2008
Assets			
Current Assets			
Cash & Equivalents	3,287,000	2,884,000	1,774,000
Short Term investments	14,135,000	10,558,000	7,778,000
Net Receivables	2,335,000	2,109,000	2,073,000
Inventory	2,022,000	2,220,000	2,075,000
Other Current Assets	1,350,000	1,161,000	1,521,000
Total Current Assets	$ 23,830,000	$ 1,161,000	$ 1,521,000
Property Plant & Equipment	5,522,000	5,738,000	5,879,000
Goodwill	11,334,000	11,335,000	11,339,000
Intangible Assets	2,230,000	2,567,000	2,988,000
Other Assets	1,271,000	1,057,000	1,016,000
Total Assets	$ 43,486,000	$ 39,629,000	$ 36,443,000
Liabilities			
Current Liabilities			
Accounts Payable	4,082,000	3,873,000	3,886,000
Short / Current Long Term Debt	2488,000		1,000,000
Total Current Liabilities	$ 6,570,000	$ 3,873,000	$ 4,886,000
Long Term Debt	10,874,000	10,601,000	9,176,000
Other Liabilities	2,098,000	2,488,000	1,995,000
Total Liabilities	$ 19,542,00	$ 16,962,000	$ 16,057,000
Stockholder's Equity			
Common Stock	27,299,000	26,944,000	25,527,000
Retained Earnings	(3,508,000)	(4,322,000)	(5,528,000)
Other Stockholder Equity	153,000	45,000	117,000
Total Stockholder Equity	$ 23,944,000	$ 22,667,000	$ 20,386,000
Total Liabilities & Stockholder Equity	$ 43,486,000	$ 39,629,000	$ 36,443,000

71 http://finance.yahoo.com/q/bs?s=AMGN+Balance+Sheet&annual

As with the income statement, balance sheets follow fairly specific formats that are in accordance with Generally Accepted Accounting Principles (GAAP). These are rules set by an independent body that provide investors with a sense of security that companies must follow strict reporting standards to ensure confidence in the investment community.

As you can see from this financial statement, assets and liabilities are segregated into two components: current and non-current. The demarcation point between the two categories is typically one year. Current assets are those items that add value to the corporation that can be readily converted into cash. These include cash on hand, accounts receivables (uncollected sales), and inventory (raw materials and finished goods not yet sold to the public) among others. Current liabilities on the other hand represent obligations of the company that will be coming due in less than one year. These items include accounts payable (debts to various vendors), and the current portion of long term debt among others. The latter represents the portion of long term loans that are expected to be paid to the creditor within one year. The relationship between current assets and current liabilities is very important. If the difference between the two is positive, that indicates that the company has enough cash and cash equivalents on hand to handle all short term obligations. This is typically a good sign because it indicates that a company has sufficient **liquidity** on hand to prevent a situation where it cannot meet bills as they come due which could result in bankruptcy. One caveat: If the positive ratio between current assets and liabilities is largely driven by inventories (a current asset), it may be masking a problem, because inventories might be more difficult to convert into cash than the term "current" asset might imply, leaving the company in a difficult position as it seeks to meet its short term obligations.

Non-current or long term assets are those items that add to the value of a corporation but are not considered to be cash equivalents. For instance, the building and property belonging to the company would not be considered items a company would sell and convert into cash to meet upcoming obligations. Intangible assets are another category of assets which you cannot see or touch but increase the overall value of the company. An example would be intellectual property; this would include patents on inventions the company has created and that are expected to add to the overall income stream of the company in the future, but can hardly be considered physical assets.

Long term liabilities can come in various forms but the item typically present in this category is **long term debt**, which comprises the total sum of loans and bonds the company owes various creditors and bondholders. As noted earlier, the portion of the loan balances that come due in less than one year are categorized as current liabilities. The interest owed on the loans is an income statement line item that falls below the operating profit line.

Once all assets and liabilities have been netted out, the resulting balance is the company's net worth, which is comprised of several components. First, the capital stock line item represents the value of all stock issued to investors at its original or par value. Unlike your statement of personal net worth, this line item is not recorded at its market value, because to do so would violate one of the principle rules of GAAP which is conservatism. The second and arguably the most important component of the company's net worth is **retained earnings**. These include the sum total of net income after taxes that have not been paid to shareholders in the form of dividends.

The next section will focus on how to make sense of corporate financial data as reflected in the company's Income Statement and Balance Sheet. We will use several ratios or metrics to try and make sense of the data, in order to determine how expensive or cheap a company's stock price might be at a given point in time. The ratios will act as "lowest common denominators"; that is, data points that are easily compared to other peers, the industry at large and the company's prior performance.

Ratio Description	Formula	Ratio Type	Purpose
Price to Earnings (P/E)	Stock Price / Earnings per Share	Valuation	How expensive is the stock price relative to its ability to generate net income / profits
Price to Sales (P/S)	Stock Price / Sales per Share	Valuation	How expensive is the stock price relative to its ability to generate sales
Price to Book (P/B)	Stock Price / Net Worth per Share	Valuation	How expensive is the stock price relative to its net worth
P/E to Earnings Growth (PEG)	Price / EPS / Earnings Growth Estimate	Valuation	How expensive is the stock price relative to its future earnings potential
Current Ratio (C/R)	Current Assets / Current Liabilities	Liquidity	Ability to meet S-T obligations
Average Collection Period (ACP)	Accounts Receivable / (Sales / 365)	Liquidity	How efficient is management at converting sales to cash?
Debt	Total Debt / Total Assets	Leverage	What percentage of the asset base is financed with debt as opposed to equity?
Times Interest Earned	Operating Income / Interest Expense	Leverage	Ability to meet interest obligations
Gross Margin	Gross Profit / Sales	Efficiency	How many cents on the $ left after direct costs accounted for?
Operating Margin	Operating Profit / Sales	Efficiency	How many cents on the $ left after recurring costs accounted for?
Net Margin	Net Income / Sales	Efficiency	How many cents on the $ left after all costs accounted for?
Return on Equity (RoE)	Net Income / Stockholders Equity	Profitability	How much income is management generating from invested capital?
Return on Assets (RoA)	Net Income / Total Assets	Profitability	How well is management employing assets to deliver profits to shareholders?

RATIO ANALYSIS

Let's assume the Smith family is interested in purchasing stock in Amgen Corporation. Amgen is a very successful pharmaceutical / biotechnology company whose common stock currently sells for approximately $54 per share. How do they approach deciding whether the investment is a proper one? The first thing to do is understand certain **qualitative** aspects of the company. For instance, what does the company produce and sell? What industry is it in? Who are its competitors? What makes this company more attractive to you than its peers? Is it a young company that appears to be growing its sales and earnings faster than the average company? Is it a mature company with more stable revenue streams and therefore a safer investment for the short, medium and long term? Has the company hired a new management team due to poor performance by the previous regime? Is the company about to launch a new product line that will excite the public and the investment community? These are just a few of the questions they will need to answer before entering into more detailed **quantitative** research as described below. **Please note all data that feeds these ratios in from the year ended 2010.**

VALUATION RATIOS

Right from the beginning, the Smith's should be asking the question, "At $54 per share (4/5/11), is the stock price too expensive (overvalued)? Is it cheap (undervalued)? Is it fairly priced? To answer this question, we need to remember that a stock price represents a claim on future earnings of the company. Therefore, Amgen's ability to grow its profits and cash flows in the future should have a direct impact on the price of the stock; presently, financial analysts expect profits per share (EPS) to grow at an estimated 7.4% compounded annual growth rate. The ratio box on the previous page lists 4 key valuation ratios. When evaluating these, you should always compare these at least to its peers (Johnson & Johnson ~$60 per share) and the overall industry to put the metric in context. Let's look at them individually:

- **Price / Earnings per Share (P/E) – Stock Price / (Net income / Total Outstanding Shares)**
  - Question answered: How much are investors willing to pay for $1 of profit **per share?**
  - Amgen P/E: $54 / (4,627,000 / 932,450) = **10.88x EPS;** 5 Year Range: 15x – 37.5x
  - Peer: Johnson & Johnson 12.5x EPS; Industry: 14.7x EPS
  - Conclusion: P/E is < than its peer, the industry and its 5 year range – **seems cheap!!**
- **Price / Sales per Share (P/S) – Stock Price / (Sales / Total Outstanding Shares)**
  - Question answered: How enthused are investors about revenue growth prospects?
  - Amgen P/S: $54 / (15,053,000 / 932,450) = **3.3x SPS**
  - Peer: Johnson & Johnson 2.7x SPS
  - Conclusion: Mature firms generally trade at levels <2; neither seems cheap on this metric
- **Price / Book Value per Share (P/B) – Stock Price / (Net Worth / Total Outstanding Shares)**
  - Question answered: What is the value the market places on the net worth of the firm?
  - Amgen P/B: $54 / (23,944,000 / 932,450) = **2.1x BVPS**
  - Peer: Johnson & Johnson 2.9x BVPS
  - Conclusion: Near or below book value (~1.0x), companies **may** present a bargain
- **P/E / EPS Growth (PEG) – P/E Ratio / Expected Earnings per Share Growth Estimates**

- o Question answered: Premium market puts on stock relative to expected future profits
- o Amgen PEG: $10.88 / 7.4^{72} = 1.4x$
- o Peer: Johnson & Johnson 2.0x
- o Conclusion: While the P/E seems cheap relative to its peers and its own trading range, analysts don't expect much profit growth from Amgen – could still be considered cheap!

LIQUIDITY RATIOS

While Amgen may appear to be selling at a relatively inexpensive price of $54 on a **valuation** basis, the Smith's should be asking the question, "Is Amgen fiscally sound?" To answer this question, the Smith's should turn their focus to the **Balance Sheet**; to reiterate, this financial statement addresses the value of the company at a **specific point in time**, by totaling the firm's assets and deducting all of its debts or liabilities. Because "cash is king", additional emphasis is placed on a firm's ability to generate cash, and pay off any bills due in an imminent timeframe. The ratio box at the beginning of this section lists 2 key liquidity ratios. When evaluating these, you should always compare these at least to its peers and the overall industry to put the metric in context. Let's look at them individually:

- **Current Ratio (C/R) – Current Assets / Current Liabilities**
  - o Question answered: Sufficient cash equivalents to meet all S-T obligations?

---

72   http://finance.yahoo.com/q/ae?s=AMGN+Analyst+Estimates

- o Amgen C/R: $23,129,000 / $6,570,000 = 3.5x
- o Peer: Johnson and Johnson: 2.0x
- o Conclusion: Not only does Amgen have enough liquidity to meet S-T needs, they exceed its total liabilities – they are "flush" in cash!!
- **Average Collection Period (ACP) – Accounts Receivable / (Sales / 365)**
  - o Question answered: How long does it take the firm to collect its credit sales?
  - o Amgen ACP: $2,335,000 / ($15,053,000/365) = **56.6 days**
  - o Peer: Johnson and Johnson: 71.1 days
  - o Conclusion: While neither collects on their credit sales very quickly, it is the nature of the industry that **large $ sales may take ~2 months to collect – no concerns at this time!**

LEVERAGE / DEBT RATIOS

Initial signs are positive for the Smith's with respect to the Balance Sheet for Amgen. The company appears to have plenty of cash on hand, and its operations appear to generate significant additional cash if its income statement profits are any indication. As they continue to examine the Balance Sheet, their focus should turn towards the company's debt position. Debt represents **risk**. Remember that a company can finance its expansion in numerous ways. Among these are: a) **stock** issues to the public (investors become owners in the company) b) **debt / bond** issues to the public (investors become lenders to the company) c) **organic growth** (company finances its growth through profits reinvested in the company) d) **other borrowing** (loans from banks and other financial institutions).

Remember that bondholders are paid in two ways. They receive periodic coupon (interest) payments and a return of their entire invested principal when the bond matures, assuming they haven't sold the bond in the interim. If a company chooses to finance its operations with debt, it acknowledges that it will periodically have to pay bondholders **fixed** interest payments as part of the promise made to them when the bond was first issued. The risk lies in that even if the company's operations suffer, and their revenues and profits correspondingly decrease, the company is still **liable for the full interest obligation** on the outstanding bonds. There are several ways to measure a company's leverage. We will review two of them below:

- **Debt Ratio (D/R) – Total Debt / Total Assets**
    - o Question answered: How does the company finance their asset growth?
    - o Amgen D/R: $19,542,000 / $43,486,000 = 44.9%
    - o Peer: Johnson and Johnson: 45.0%
    - o Conclusion: < $1 of every $2 of asset value is debt related for Amgen. **No concern here!**
- **Times Interest Earned (TIE) – Earnings Before Interest & Taxes / Interest Expense**
    - o Question answered: Firm's ability to meet interest obligations.
    - o Amgen TIE: $5,921,000 / $604,000 = 9.8x
    - o Peer: Johnson and Johnson: 38.2x

o Conclusion: Both companies generate significant amount of income from their operations to cover all interest obligations – **no concern here!**

EFFICIENCY RATIOS

Prospective investors often times will make the statement "I want to own stocks of well managed companies". What does that mean? Do you know the CEO's and CFO's of the companies you will buy stock in? Not likely! How do you make a performance judgment other than looking at whether the stock price has risen significantly in the past months or years? If you wait until the stock has risen sharply before you purchase, chances are you will have missed out on a good investment opportunity, in which the foreseeable future may have more downside possibilities (stock price drops) than upside opportunities (stock price rises).

Up to this point we have determined that the price of Amgen's stock does not seem excessive on a "per share" basis relative to its earnings (net income), sales, net worth and its expected earnings growth rate. In addition, they appear to have a solid balance sheet indicating a stable, well run business with significant amounts of cash and manageable debt levels. It is important to note that when running a business, **management's operational goal is to produce greater amounts of goods and services at a cheaper cost per unit, also referred to as achieving "economies of scale".** This is how you drive greater and greater earnings per share growth. Management can track their progress in meeting this goal through **margin performance**. Following are three ratios the Smith's should evaluate:

- **Gross Margin (GM) – Gross Profit / Revenue**
  - Question answered: Total "cents / $" remaining after all **"direct"** costs are deducted
  - Amgen GM: $12,833,000 / $15,053,000 = 85.3%
  - Peer: Johnson and Johnson: 69.5%
  - Conclusion: Amgen's direct cost structure (labor, materials, overhead) is very small affording it sizeable profit generating potential
- **Operating Margin (OM) – Operating Income / Revenue**
  - Question answered: Total "cents / $" remaining after all **"recurring"** costs are deducted
  - Amgen GM: $5,545,000 / $15,053,000 = 36.8%
  - Peer: Johnson and Johnson: 26.8%
  - Conclusion: Amgen's indirect / operating cost structure is sizeable; however, R&D costs are included here which are necessary to ensure long term product development; also, they are still more efficient than J&J, reflecting that Amgen is not just a mature pharmaceutical firm, but retains traits of the more fast growing Biotechnology industry.
- **Net Profit Margin (NM) – Net Income After Taxes / Revenue**
  - Question answered: Total "cents / $" remaining after **all** costs are deducted
  - Amgen NM: $4,627,000 / $15,053,000 = 30.7%
  - Peer: Johnson and Johnson: 21.7%

    o Conclusion: **Amgen is able to generate 30 cents in profit for every sales $ - amazingly efficient for a company this large!**

PROFITABILITY RATIOS

Thus far, we have determined through the valuation ratios that Amgen's stock price does not appear expensive and in fact could be considered a good "value" given its earnings today and its profit potential in the future. The Balance Sheet appears strong given Amgen's strong liquidity position, its ability to pay its current interest obligations and the fact that its debt levels don't indicate excessive risk being undertaken by management. From a cost control perspective, Amgen's business model and management acumen reflect a company with significant margin generating potential, especially when compared to one of its biggest rivals. Now we need to investigate one more area of performance; that is, how well does the company generate profits from both its invested capital (stock sales + retained earnings from its operations), and its overall asset base. In essence, how well does it use the resources at its disposal to generate net income to grow the company? Following are two key metrics to help sort this out:

- **Return on Equity (ROE) – Net Income After Taxes / Stockholders Equity (Net Worth)**
  - o Question answered: Profits generated from invested capital?
  - o Amgen ROE: $4,627,000 / $23,944,000 = 19.3%
  - o Peer: Johnson and Johnson: 23.7%

- o Conclusion: **Although Amgen's return on invested capital is < its peer enjoys, anything approaching 20% ROE should be considered outstanding!**
- **Return on Assets (ROA) – Net Income After Taxes / Total Assets**
  - o Question answered: Profits generated from deployed asset base?
  - o Amgen ROE: $4,627,000 / $43,486,000 = 10.6%
  - o Peer: Johnson and Johnson: 13.0%
  - o Conclusion: **Amgen has deployed its assets in a more than adequate fashion, although JNJ enjoys even better results for the last 12 months.**

So where does this leave us? We have compared Amgen's 2010 results with those of Johnson and Johnson. The two are considered peers although no one would confuse the latter with being a key member of the Biotechnology community. They are more of a pharmaceutical company in the classical terms that define that industry. Amgen began as a small biotechnology firm that through the successful introduction of revolutionary medical treatments, quickly catapulted itself to be one of the leading companies providing advanced treatments for cancer and other debilitating diseases.

It appears that on the surface, Amgen's stock price appears to be selling at relatively inexpensive levels compared to its peer. It has solid balance sheet and income statement results that allow a prospective investor to feel more comfortable with investing precious dollars in this company. I would like to caution that although ratios serve a key function in dissecting a company's performance for the purpose of determining investment viability, one should study the company more thoroughly before investing. I would encourage investors to read the company's security filings (i.e., 10K, 10Q, etc...) to understand what management has to say about the performance of the company and to understand what potential risks lie ahead that are the focus of the company's managerial team. In addition, I would urge you to use these same metrics and compare the company to its prior performance. How do these ratios stack up against 2009, 2008 and prior years? The point being, that just like you would invest time and resources determining which car or major appliance you would purchase, the Smith's should spend at least the same amount of time and effort studying their investment opportunities prior to allocating significant amounts of risk capital into those investments.

Summary / Tips to Remember
- Investing for one's retirement through "tax deferred" savings accounts (i.e.; 401K, 403B IRA) should be taking place from the very beginning
- Investing in "taxable" accounts should likely wait until after total debt balances have either been eliminated or reduced to a manageable level
- If investing in individual equities, a detailed fundamental analysis of the stock in question should

be undertaken to include the use of many different types of ratios / metrics

- Mutual funds diversify an investor's risk by spreading the investment over a basket of different stocks; they are priced according to their Net Asset Value at the close of each business day.
- Exchange Traded Funds (ETFs) allow the public to invest in different sectors, countries, industries, etc... They are priced as if they were individual common stocks.

(N) NURSING / LONG-TERM CARE

By the time the Smith's reach their late forties, as long as their financial house is in order, chances are they will have a budget they employ consistently to prioritize expenses; they should have a plan in place to pay down any debt outstanding, and will have purchased a home and earned significant equity in it, and found the means to invest money both in a tax-deferred savings account and in other taxable instruments. Should they have adequate levels of income (salaries), they may even have money set aside for college educations, weddings, and other big-ticket obligations. Just when life appears to be clicking on all cylinders and a comfortable retirement is on the horizon, it becomes apparent that long-term care and daily living costs (custodial costs) could pose a major obstacle that has the potential to cripple even the most financially sound households. As a result, more and more people are considering purchasing insurance or protection for this future cost, and it is for this reason that I consider it to be the fifth cornerstone of the financial freedom foundation.

What is **Long-Term Care (LTC) insurance**? It is insurance or financial protection that is purchased to help defray the costs of assistance with activities of daily living, such as bathing, dressing, and eating. It also includes the kind of care one would need should they be afflicted with a severe cognitive impairment like Alzheimer's. Depending on the Long Term Care plan purchased, it may cover skilled, intermediate, and custodial care in the home, an adult day-care center, an assisted living facility, a nursing home, or a hospice facility. Some plans, such as the Federal Long Term Care Insurance Program, also cover home care from informal providers such as friends, neighbors, and family members who didn't normally live with you at the time you became eligible for benefits.[73]

Although many Americans currently do not even have traditional health insurance, most individuals that do have it obtain their care through policies provided by employers or purchased individually. Traditional insurance tends to cover all or part of the cost incurred from doctor visits, prescriptions, hospitalization, and surgical procedures. One of the biggest medical misconceptions is that traditional healthcare policies will automatically include long-term custodial care coverage. In addition, many individuals assume Medicare and Medicaid, which are federal government programs providing healthcare to the elderly, will cover long-term custodial care. Medicare and Medicaid supplement insurance (also referred to as Medi-Gap because it provides stopgap coverage for most health issues not covered under traditional Medicare policies) cover catastrophic illnesses; in addition, they provide for hospitalization, physician visits, and, beginning in 2004, provide prescription coverage along with **very**

---

73   http://www.ltcfeds.com/programdetails/typecarecovered.html

limited nursing home care, usually for skilled nursing needs. They **do not** provide coverage for daily living or custodial needs. Medicaid is medical insurance for the impoverished; it has guidelines set at the federal level but is managed by the states, who tailor services according to their respective needs. As such, there is significant taxpayer money spent at both the federal and state level. To qualify, recipients must spend down virtually all their assets, at which time they will receive the medical and custodial care they require.

Long-term care insurance is a relatively new phenomenon. In previous generations, individuals took care of the elderly within their families. Most families could count on a younger relative living near their elderly parents or grandparents to provide them with the care and assistance necessary to allow them to remain in their homes or to move in with them until they passed away. In addition, many women did not work outside the home, which enabled the family to have additional help for the elderly members. With the advent of two-working-parent households and families whose offspring all live in different cities, the elderly do not have the luxury of always having loved ones nearby to assist them in their daily custodial needs once they begin losing the ability to fend for themselves. As such, long-term care insurance has evolved to fill this vacuum that previously did not exist.

If long-term care needs are not anticipated properly, they may represent a staggering financial drain on your family's estate. In 2010, average (private room) nursing home stays averaged approximately $229 per day. This equates to approximately $6,870 per month or roughly

$84,000 annually.[74] **An average nursing home stay of 29 months can result in unplanned expenses of more than $200,000.** This could cripple a household's net worth! By 2030, it is estimated that average annual nursing home costs could exceed $190,000 assuming a 5 percent annual increase in healthcare costs continues.[75]

Long-term care comes in many different forms, but following are some of the more common types of long-term care assistance.

- **Nursing Home Care** provides round-the-clock nursing assistance in an established facility.
- **Assisted Living** is a scaled-down version of nursing home assistance, emphasizing daily help with food preparation and medication dispensation, and other activities of daily living.
- **Adult Day Care** provides seniors with activities and companionship during a given day.
- **Home Health Care** entails time-limited nursing assistance in the home for activities of daily living.
- **Hospice Care** provides nursing, social work, and spiritual assistance for terminally ill patients with less than six months of life expectancy in the home, nursing home, or hospice facility.
- **Respite Care** provides for short-term assistance to caretakers who desire a temporary rest from the

---

74 http://www.smartmoney.com/personal-finance/retirement/how-to-pick-the-right-nursing-home-1301445831107/

75 http://www.retirement-living.com/article/17/nursing-home-costs-could-reach-190k-a-year-by-2030

responsibility; for example, a caregiver who wants to go on vacation for a week can obtain a short stay in a nursing home for their patient while they are on vacation.

Daily costs for these services vary significantly, and each family needs to make the choice of which type of care is best suited for them given their current health and budget. For example, the average annual cost for home health care approximated $44,000 in 2010[76], which was calculated based on ~44 hours per week of assistance. These costs may be prohibitive for most households, but indicative of the staggering costs the elderly currently face for health care. It is expected that more than half of all women and a third of all men above the age of sixty-five will spend some time in a nursing home prior to their deaths. In fact, 43 percent of Americans age sixty-five or older will spend some time in a nursing home, and as previously stated, the average nursing home stay is just under two and one-half years.[77]

Before we hit the panic button, this statistic needs to be clarified. At any given time, only a small percentage of the elderly population in the United States resides in a nursing home facility.[78] These statistics indicate a likelihood that long-term care expenses will be a significant financial burden for most Americans at some point in time. Proper planning for this need is essential if a family wishes to maintain

---

76   http://www.kaiserhealthnews.org/Daily-Reports/2010/April/28/
      Home-Health-Care-Costs.aspx

77   http://www.investopedia.com/articles/04/112904.asp

78   http://www.efmoody.com/longterm/nursingstatistics.html

the value of their estate for their heirs. The table below provides some additional perspective on this.

EACH OF THESE RISKS MAY RESULT IN A LOSS OF $100,000 OR MORE
Home Destroyed by Fire - 1 chance in 1,200
Auto Accident Liability Suit - 1 chance in 240
Major Medical Expense - 1 chance in 15
Major Long Term Care Expense - 1 chance in 2

source: Underwriters Long Term Care Council, 2002

Most people want to avoid lengthy nursing home stays. They can be depressing and for many patients, even degrading, as some individuals begin losing some of their dignity given that daily bodily functions are often completed with someone else's assistance. It is for this reason that many individuals are opting for professional assistance inside their own home. As you have seen earlier in this section, no matter what type of custodial care you end up choosing, it may result in out-of-pocket expenditures which range from $30,000 to $80,000 annually, depending on the level of assistance. Recent history reflects that these costs have risen by about 4 percent annually.[79]

---

79   http://news.yahoo.com/s/usnews/20110510/ts_usnews/
    costoflongtermcarerisesininstitutionsstaysflatathome

How do we prepare for this likely expenditure down the road? As I mentioned at the outset of this section, by the time you reach your late forties you should begin thinking seriously of purchasing a long-term care policy for you and your spouse. This policy will enable a husband and wife to establish the financing for their own custodial needs while relieving their children of this future financial burden and preserving the overall value of their estate. As recently as 2007, average annual long term care insurance plans averaged about $2,000 annually, or $165 per month for household participants aged 50-59.[80] Depending on the type of long term care insurance plan the Smith household opts for, the plans can range between $1000 and $3000 per year. **The way to approach this is as follows: it is much better to spend approximately $2,000 to $3,000 annually (an amount one can budget) than it is to begin spending $75,000 to $85,000 annually out of pocket for nursing home services if you have no long term care option.** Although the insurance may appear somewhat expensive, there is a chance that it will actually become more affordable as the popularity increases and the total cost of providing custodial care is spread among that many more participants.

As with any relatively new financial plan, there are some caveats. Anecdotal evidence indicates that in recent years, some dissatisfaction exists with LTC plans. For instance, consumer advocates and state regulators say that terms and features vary widely, from when benefits start and the maximum daily payout to how long benefits last and what

---

80   http://www.longtermcare.gov/LTC/Main_Site/Paying_LTC/
Private_Programs/LTC_Insurance/index.aspx#LTCICRB

services are covered[81]. In addition, state insurance regulators field a steady stream of complaints from consumers over issues such as unexpected premium increases and denial of coverage. These drawbacks obviously affect credibility. If long term care insurance plans are to become ubiquitous in the marketplace, gaining consumer trust will be paramount to their success long term.

Summary / Tips to Remember
- 33% of men, 50% of women will spend time in a nursing home; planning for this cost is essential
- Long Term Care insurance should be considered in ones 50s and 60s – neither Medicare, Medicaid, nor Social Security will provide for daily living costs which can cripple net worth
- Long Term Care insurance is still in immature market – as such, one must be diligent in ensuring that your plan covers the assistance you are seeking and that premiums don't spike up arbitrarily.

---

81   http://www.over50web.net/finance/pros-and-cons-of-long-term-care-insurance/

(D) ESTATE PLANNING/DEATH PREPARATION

The common theme running throughout this book is that the key to financial freedom for most Americans lies in proper planning and self-discipline. While most of us may never achieve complete financial independence and will still need to work for a living, we can still generate a hefty retirement nest egg by following the principles laid out in the previous sections. Once the household debt has been eliminated or significantly reduced, and enough savings have been generated (through tax deferred savings plans and taxable accounts) to fund the retirement nest egg while ensuring that a sufficient reserve has been set aside to satisfy large future obligations (think long term care insurance), one key remaining piece to the completion of the personal financial puzzle is to ensure that the value of the estate will be protected.

The goal of estate planning, which is the sixth pillar of the financial freedom structure, is to provide for the well-being of one's heirs and to distribute the value of the estate in such a way as to ensure that the objectives of the owner of the estate are met during life and after the individual's death. All families wish to provide for the well-being of their heirs. It is part of the natural order of life that the current generation wants its children to have at least the same if not greater opportunities than it enjoyed. I will not begin to address all the items within the estate planning lexicon, but I will focus on the following areas that are among the most critical to the preservation of accumulated wealth and the seamless transition of assets from members of one generation to another:

WILLS

These documents represent the legal means to transfer the proceeds of estates to the selected beneficiaries. This is not just a mechanism to protect wealthy people. Wills are essential to ensuring that one's wishes regarding asset distribution are granted after death. If a person of any significant means dies without an official will, it is referred to as dying **intestate,** and it will be left up to the courts to determine the best method of distributing the proceeds of any estate left behind. This is obviously not the ideal solution as it fails to take into account the deceased's wishes. Even if the estate owner leaves behind an official will, the courts usually will still become involved to certify that the will is in fact executed properly, reflecting the most up to date wishes of the owner, and that he or she was legally competent at the time the will was created. This process is referred to as **probate** and its purpose is to place an official stamp on the wishes of the deceased. The process involves conducting a full and final accounting of the estate to ensure all assets are tabulated and all debts are paid. In addition, the goal is to ensure that the intended beneficiaries receive the proceeds due them according to the will. As one would expect, this process can be cumbersome and costly, which is why many households of significant means look to avoid it.

Not everyone needs a will, but a good rule of thumb is that when you have children you should begin the process of creating the means to provide for them should you and your spouse die prematurely. In addition, the birth of your offspring also presents you with the responsibility of selecting guardians for the children in the case of an untimely death. A typical will can cost less than a thousand dollars to create and will normally be executed by an estate attorney. The cost will undoubtedly rise for wealthier individuals whose estates traditionally are much more complex, consisting of many differing types of assets.

Not all assets are subject to probate. Only those assets held in the decedent's name (the deceased party) without designated beneficiaries when death occurs are to be "probated". There are four key types of assets that will be passed on to named beneficiaries outside of the probate process:

- Property held by the decedent and a spouse as JTWROS (Joint Tenant with Right of Survivorship) – e.g. a taxable investment account held in both your and your spouse's name
- Property held in a trust

- Accounts Payable on Death (POD) or Transferred on Death (TOD) to named heirs – e.g. a bank account payable on death to a decedent's child, and even IRAs to be transferred on death to heirs
- Insurance or retirement proceeds payable to a beneficiary on the occasion of the decedent's death

REVOCABLE / IRREVOCABLE TRUSTS

These documents are similar to wills, but have some key advantages that make them an enticing option for individuals. A revocable living trust is a written declaration and contract in which you state that you (as *settlor*) are transferring your property into a revocable living trust for the benefit of yourself during your lifetime (lifetime beneficiary) and after your passing, for the benefit of your heirs (remainder beneficiaries). You will be the **trustee** of your revocable living trust, which means that during your lifetime, you will have complete control over the revocable living trust's assets. The **successor trustee** you name will take control over your revocable living trust in case of your death or incapacity. In addition, you will have the power to change, amend, or revoke your revocable living trust at any time during your lifetime.[82]

The main advantage of a revocable living trust is the avoidance of probate. Most wills are probated; not so with a revocable living trust. Since probate only affects assets you own personally at the time of your death, assets placed in a revocable living trust are not owned by you, but instead by the trust. Therefore, there is no probate or validation of those

---

82 http://www.mobar.org/9c8206ad-c515-4114-806a-a3531d9297a9.aspx

assets. **Probate will generally cost about 1 to 2 percent of the value of the probated assets and may take anywhere from several weeks up to a couple of years (absent litigation or contested claims) to complete.** You can save probate fees by using a properly funded revocable living trust.[83]

Since probate is a court proceeding, your will and the valuation of your assets are open to public inspection. A revocable living trust, however, is confidential and the transfer of assets from the revocable living trust is kept from public view. When the **settlor** of a revocable living trust dies or becomes incapacitated, the successor trustee continues the administration of the revocable living trust. With a revocable living trust, there is no gap period between the time of death and the appointment of the executor, which occurs under a will. Also, the continuity of the revocable living trust is preserved through the successor trustee if the **settlor** becomes incapacitated through illness or accident. In this case, the revocable living trust would be administered for the benefit of the grantor.[84]

Initially a trust has greater costs with respect to its formation and implementation than a will, but those costs are usually a small percentage of the amount saved through the avoidance of probate costs at the time the grantor dies. Additionally, if confidentiality and continuity of ownership are important objectives, then the trust is the document of choice. Conversely, if confidentiality and continuity are not important objectives, and if the initial cost and administration of a

---

83   Ibid

84   Ibid

trust outweigh the potential savings through the avoidance of probate, then a will should be used.[85]

An irrevocable trust differs from the revocable type in that the grantor of the assets usually transfers ownership and control of property during his lifetime. It typically constitutes giving the property to the trust. The trust then stands as a **separate taxable entity** and pays tax on its accumulated income. Irrevocable trusts typically receive preferential tax treatment. Since this type of trust involves lack of ownership and control of the property being transferred to the trust, it has limited appeal to most taxpayers.[86] In addition, the details of this trust alternative include fairly advanced income tax avoidance schemes that do not typically benefit most taxpayers. **One significant benefit to irrevocable living trusts is their potential immunity from estate tax considerations.** Property that you place in an irrevocable trust is no longer considered part of your estate, meaning that the property typically isn't included in your estate's value when it comes to determining if you owe death taxes and, if so, how much.[87]

INSURANCES
LIFE INSURANCE

Although I incorporate the discussion of life insurance under the estate planning umbrella, it is a financial instrument that should be purchased fairly early in life. In its

85   Ibid
86   http://www.investopedia.com/terms/i/irrevocabletrust.asp
87   http://www.dummies.com/how-to/content/revocable-versus-
      irrevocable-trusts.html

simplest form, life insurance is the **purchase of protection against loss of income**. Whether you have just purchased a home, are recently married, or had your first child, life insurance is essential to protecting your assets and ensuring that your loved ones are provided for in case of an untimely death. In addition, it takes care of paying funeral expenses, which is the last thing a grief-stricken family wants to be bothered with when a loved one passes away. Purchasing the right type and the right amount of life insurance can be a formidable endeavor, particularly because there are a myriad of products in the marketplace targeted at all sorts of demographics, risk tolerances, etc.

In essence, life insurance guarantees the protection of one's assets through the payment of periodic payments or **premiums** by the owner of the life insurance policy. At the time of the policyholder's death, the insurance company will pay the face value of the policy to the policyholder's designated beneficiaries. For example, if Steve Smith purchases a $250,000 life insurance policy, Susan would be the most likely beneficiary and she would receive the entire payment tax-free as long as all premium payments were up to date at the time of his death. Regardless of which of the many different life insurance products you purchase, certain factors will hold true in virtually all cases:

- The younger one is at the time the life insurance policy is purchased, the cheaper the periodic premium payment owed to the insurance company. The reason is that the company is expecting the policyholder to live long enough that, even if they have to pay out the entire principal amount to the designated beneficiary, the total will be offset by the sum of the premium payments made by the policyholder over time. Time value of money also enters the discussion, since future life insurance proceeds will be worth less than they are today due to inflationary impacts in future years. Conversely, the older one is when entering into a life insurance contract, the higher the premium payments will be for the same principal amount, as the insurance company will have to charge higher premiums for a shorter time span in order to generate a profit on the sale of that policy. Profit, after all, is a key reason insurance companies are in business and able to provide this benefit.

- Healthier individuals will pay less for the same policy as those in the same age bracket who have a history of severe illnesses. As an example, smokers will pay more than non-smokers for similar policies since the incidence of lung cancer is much higher among those who smoke.

There are many different types of life insurance products and hybrids of life insurance. It would be too lengthy and counter-productive to mention them all in detail. The intent is to convey the message that life insurance is an essential component of your personal finance portfolio. I do, however, want to comment on a key decision any individual will have to make when purchasing a life insurance policy and focus on a few of the product alternatives available in the marketplace.

WHOLE vs TERM LIFE INSURANCE

Term Life: This life insurance product guarantees a death benefit lump sum payment to designated beneficiaries at the time of the policyholder's death, in exchange for an annual payment better known as the **premium**. This product is meant to protect a household against loss of income for a relatively small annual fee and is not meant to provide households with a wealth producing vehicle. Wealth creation is reserved for assets that produce significant annual rates of return, such as primary residences, stocks, bonds, mutual funds, etc...

TYPES of TERM PLANS[88]:

- Renewable Term – in place for a specified term and can be renewed without the insured having to provide proof of good health each time
- Level Term – fixed coverage with stable premiums over a set period of time (usually – 5-10 year increments)
- Decreasing Term – premiums remain level but the amount of coverage decreases throughout term
- Convertible – ability to change to a permanent type of life insurance without a medical exam, although the premiums will likely rise
- Return of Premium – ability to recover your premium if the policy term expires without cashing in on the face value – premiums however, will be higher than regular term plans

---

88   http://www.aig.com/Types-ofTerm-Life-Insurance_20_26009.html

JACK D. LETZER JR.

HOW MUCH LIFE INSURANCE COVERAGE is ENOUGH?

Let's assume Steve Smith is in his early 30s, and is a relatively healthy individual who does not smoke. Chances are a $250,000 term life policy would only cost him somewhere in the neighborhood of ~$200 per year, or ~$15 - ~$17 per month. This is a nominal amount that could be considered a miscellaneous cost in one's monthly budget. If Susan Smith is of a similar age, they might consider taking out a policy for each of them and the monthly premiums will approximately double, still fitting within a monthly budget (although she will likely enjoy a slightly smaller premium due to the fact that they live longer).

So now the Smith's have $500K worth of life insurance protection, at a relatively small monthly cost. Should they have $1,000,000 of coverage? $2,000,000? $100,000? What is the right amount? This is left up to the discretion of the couple but the following solution might work for a large number of households:

Purchase enough life insurance protection to at least pay the balance on the mortgage!

Think about it. When a major income earner passes away, the family will be dealing with unparalleled grief as well as trying to pick up the pieces from the enormous loss. They will be dealing with funeral costs, as well as significant adjustments that follow tragedy. The last thing a family needs to worry about is having to uproot children from schools, having the surviving spouse be forced to undertake an additional job to replace lost income, and potentially face a complete change in lifestyle. All those things will occur if the family is no longer able to pay for the mortgage, the largest monthly bill for the majority of homeowners.

If, however, a family is able to pay off the mortgage, it will provide the surviving spouse with the time required to make the necessary lifestyle adjustments and relieve the individual from additional heartache involved with the forced sale of the house, school changes for children, etc.. Nothing says you can't purchase additional life insurance. The Smith's may want to use part of the life insurance to set up a college fund: another large, usually unplanned expense. Husbands and wives need to discuss these issues and plan accordingly, in order to avoid terrible ramifications that may follow tragedies.

Whole Life: This insurance product guarantees a death benefit lump sum payment similar to the term life policy, but it will have a larger payout, as the death benefit will be combined with a **cash value** payout that will have accumulated over the life of the policy, in exchange for the annual premium paid by the policyholder. The policyholder can also borrow against the cash value of the policy in question.

At first glance it would appear that whole life insurance offers a more compelling reason to purchase than term life since the product includes a cash component driven by possible investment returns. However, annual premiums for whole life are **much** higher than term (8x to 10x as much), as they incorporate a hefty commission for the insurance agent who sold the policy; in addition, the policy is permanent, meaning it will be in effect for the policyholder's entire life, as long as premiums are paid in full, whereas term policies normally expire after a certain point in time. Finally, there are the cash payout and dividends generated over the lifetime of the policy that are used to entice investors.

Those who tout whole life policies claim they constitute a forced savings account. Whole life policyholders end up spending relatively large sums of money for the annual premium compared to term life policyholders, expecting a large payout for their beneficiaries at the time of their death. This line of thinking would indicate that whole life policies achieve annual investment returns comparable to the more traditional methods of investing. However, it is very difficult to determine investment gains and losses from life insurance policies, but a good rule of thumb is that it may take fifteen to twenty years to achieve substantial cash accumulation in one's whole life policy. Two types of whole life policies that bear a little more scrutiny are a) **variable whole life** and b) **universal life** insurance.

Variable Life Insurance

This is a type of whole life policy that guarantees permanent protection to the beneficiary upon the death of the policyholder[89]. It is generally the most expensive type of cash value insurance because it allows the policyholder to allocate a portion of the premium to a separate account comprised of various investment accounts such as stocks, bonds, mutual

---

89 http://www.investopedia.com/terms/v/variablelifeinsurancepolicy. asp

funds, et. al. One advantage of this policy is that investment earnings are not taxed unless the policyholder **surrenders** or terminates the policy. Interest earned from investments may also be applied too future premiums, lowering future costs of owning the policy.

If the product exists it must benefit certain groups of people. Again, for individuals who do not save, variable whole life policies may be worth the hefty premium, since they tend to spend money as fast as it comes in, but paying the premiums will be the only way to keep the policy in force. Secondly, individuals often use whole life policies as an estate planning tool. Large estates have in the past been subject to exorbitant taxation. Whole life insurance policies have often been used to mitigate the tax exposure for the decedent's estate, since life insurance proceeds are tax free to the beneficiaries. The proceeds can then be used to help pay down the taxes.

We mentioned that whole life policies include a **guaranteed** death benefit with a cash value distribution. To fulfill that promise, insurance companies need to invest the premiums in such a way that little to no risk is assumed by the policyholder. As such, the premiums typically are invested in fixed income securities such as U.S. Treasury bonds, and cash or cash equivalents; i.e. Certificates of Deposit (CDs). As a result, annual rates of return are minimal relative to stocks, equity mutual funds and corporate bonds, since the guarantor (insurance company) has to ensure there is no loss of principal. Some investors will accept an increased level of risk, in order to achieve additional returns. That's where the variable nature of these plans comes into play, allowing investors to invest some of the premiums into instruments with **variable** rates of return, acknowledging that some loss of principal may occur as a result.

Universal Life Insurance

This policy offers a low-cost protection of term life insurance as well as a savings element (like whole life insurance) which is invested to provide a cash value buildup[90]. The death benefit, savings element and premiums can be reviewed and altered as a policyholder's circumstances change. In addition, unlike traditional whole life insurance, universal life insurance allows the policyholder to use the interest from his or her accumulated savings to help pay premiums. Universal life insurance was created to provide more flexibility than traditional whole life insurance by allowing the policy owner to shift money between the insurance and savings components of the policy. Premiums, which are variable, are broken down by the insurance company into insurance and savings, allowing the policy owner to make adjustments based on his or her individual circumstances. For example, if the savings portion is earning a low return, it can be used instead of external funds to pay the premiums. Unlike whole life insurance, universal life allows the cash value of investments to grow at a variable rate that is adjusted monthly.

Although these types of whole life policies contain attractive characteristics, I believe that life insurance policies in general should not be viewed as investment vehicles

---

90   http://www.investopedia.com/terms/u/universallife.asp

but rather as a means to protect your loved ones from the loss of income due to an untimely death. For a majority of Americans, I would recommend the following steps be taken:

LIFE INSURANCE PURCHASING RECOMMENDATIONS

• Buy a Term Life policy when you are recently married. The amount of the policy should be enough to protect the value of your assets; for example, the proceeds could be used to pay off your mortgage should the principal breadwinner die prematurely

• Invest the difference between a Term Premium and a Whole Life premium in a traditional investment vehicle such as stocks, bonds, mutual funds and real estate

• Purchase additional Term Life insurance at a later date if you feel the total coverage is insufficient

• Beware of buying too much insurance. At the end of the day, you want to protect your loved ones and pay for funeral services, but they do not need enough to retire on and go sit on a beach somewhere "living the life of Riley"

AUTOMOBILE INSURANCE

For most young Americans, the purchase of automobile insurance is one of the first key financial decisions of their lives. However, what do Americans really know about this obligation? I know from anecdotal evidence that some young people believe this monthly or periodic payment is a deposit, meaning that after some period of time, they will get their money back. WRONG!!! Automobile insurance, like all other forms of insurance is the purchase of protection against some type of loss. In this case, it is physical and financial protection against a collision, theft, or some other mishap. Before you think of passing on this coverage and saving a few dollars, you will need to remember that every state requires you to be covered under an insurance policy prior to being issued a driver's license or being allowed to purchase a car[91].

WHAT IS COVERED?

There are many components to a typical automobile insurance policy. The overall coverage, however, is broken down into two major categories: **policyholder and the automobile**. Pricing a particular policy then depends on a) how much coverage one wishes to purchase to protect oneself from damages and b) how much of a risk does the insured or those covered under the policy present to the insurance company. Following is a quick synopsis of the major components of any policy.

- **Liability** - covers personal medical expenses and the medical expenses of one's passengers
- **Collision** - covers the damage to one's vehicle – most expensive component
- **Comprehensive** - covers damage that may be caused from an event other than a collision with another vehicle such as fire, theft, floods, falling object, earthquakes, etc...
- **Uninsured Motorist** – covers one's injuries sustained in an accident with someone who is uninsured, underinsured, or a hit and run accident
- **Bodily Injury** - covers injuries received by others, legal defense costs and claims against the insured
- **Property Damage** – covers damage to other's property, legal costs and claims against the insured

---

91   http://www.careonecredit.com/Knowledge/Article.aspx?article=400

Most states require that the insured purchases a policy with a minimum amount of insurance. The purpose is to ensure that whenever accidents occur, injured parties receive proper restitution. However, the reason uninsured motorist insurance exists is that some drivers fall behind their insurance payments or stop altogether causing the insurance policies to lapse. Remember: with any insurance one is purchasing protection, so if the act of purchasing stops (i.e. paying the bills) the coverage is eliminated.

PRICING AUTO INSURANCE

Now that we know the key components of an auto insurance policy, the *premium* or the price of a policy to a consumer is based on several factors, all geared towards determining the statistical odds that an accident will occur, and that the insurance company will have to pay benefits to the injured parties. It is important to note that automobile insurance does not come in standard prices. As you can see from the following factors, insurance premiums can vary widely from consumer to consumer.

- Age – the younger one is, the odds are the insurance premium will be higher because young people are less experienced drivers and too often they tend to enjoy speeding leading to careless behavior. Unfortunately, responsible young drivers tend to get lumped in with those that are not.
- Driving record – speeding tickets, or other moving violations will significantly increase the cost of one's premiums since they directly indicate that the odds of being in a significant accident are higher.

- Coverage – the more protection one purchases for each of the key components listed above, the higher the premiums. The state one lives in will require a minimum amount of coverage but be wary of obtaining too much coverage
- Deductible – auto insurance firms want to make sure the insured pays a minimum amount for insurance in case they try to get by with minimal coverage. Should an accident occur, causing the insured to apply for insurance benefits, he will be responsible for an up-front cost before the insurance benefits kick in. The lower one's overall coverage, the higher the deductible and vice-versa. *We'll get you now or we'll get you later!*
- Replacement value – The more expensive the vehicle purchased, the greater the premium since it will cost the insurance company more money to make any necessary repairs or replace the vehicle if it is a complete loss.
- Location of domicile – where one lives has a direct impact on the premium one will be charged. For example, if the insured lives in a congested city, she will in all likelihood be charged a significantly higher premium than if she lived in a suburban or rural setting, because the odds of being involved in an accident rise dramatically in a congested area.
- Distance to work – if the insurance company believes that one's commute is of a significant amount, they may charge a higher premium because the longer and farther the drive, the greater the chances an accident or other moving violation will occur.

Automobile insurance is a must if one wishes to drive and will be a key component of the monthly budget. Driving safely and understanding the components of the insurance premium and what coverage is best suited for the insured, will contribute significantly towards better financial decision-making in this area.

PROPERTY / CASUALTY INSURANCE

Assume the Smith's have purchased life insurance, health insurance and automobile insurance and all comprise a portion of their monthly budget. Are they fully insured? Not yet, but they are getting close. One other key piece of insurance is property / casualty insurance. This product provides insurance protection for one's home and business[92], against things such as fire, theft and some weather damage. The key difference is as follows:

- Property Insurance - protects a person or business with an interest in physical property against its loss or the loss of its income-producing abilities
- Casualty insurance - protects a person or business against legal liability for losses caused by injury to other people or damage to the property of others.

Property is insured in two distinct ways, through **open perils** and **named perils**. The former provides insurance coverage for all causes of loss not specifically excluded in the policy. One common area of exclusion is due to floods. Most homeowners mistakenly believe their

---

92   http://www.iso.com/index.php?option=com_content&task=view
     &id=12&Itemid=399

standard home insurance policy covers them for loss due to floods. Unfortunately, most private insurers do not offer flood insurance due to their inability to make any money from this product. Is that true? Unfortunately, yes. Insurance companies make money by collecting premiums from many participants and paying benefits to a much smaller pool of participants. With flood insurance, there are not enough individuals paying insurance premiums to offset the catastrophic losses that too many people experience during a natural disaster such as a hurricane or flood. As a result, individuals seeking to protect homes and businesses in low lying areas against risk of flooding, are forced to purchase the insurance from the federal government, which does not have the same requirements to make a profit that a business has (they can always print money if they need to – you try that one!). A downside of having government sponsored flood insurance is that it enables bad judgment, in that people continue buying property in flood zones because the government will always be there to bail them out during a catastrophe. Contrary to open perils, named peril policies offer coverage for explicitly listed events. These policies are narrower in scope (less coverage) but are sold at a discount to open insurance policies.

For most individuals or households, they will have purchased property insurance when they purchase their home. Individuals owning small businesses or luxury items such as boats may wish to purchase additional property / casualty policies to provide all of their assets with the necessary insurance protection.

ANNUITIES

As alluded to at the outset of this section, estate planning consists of all pertinent activities associated with preparing for the transfer of one's estate (net worth) to that individual's heirs and loved ones. We have just finished discussing wills, trusts and insurance policies which are designed to protect one's wealth and to enable the most efficient transfer of the wealth to the beneficiaries. Notwithstanding these areas of estate planning, investments can play a part in the formulation of a sound estate planning strategy, particularly when it comes to generating income for retirees. Although we have discussed investments in a previous section, one investment product does exist that is more closely tied to estate planning activities than typical investment activities. These are **annuities**! The reason for this distinction is that annuities are typically purchased from insurance companies and not investment companies[93].

HOW DO THEY WORK?

An annuity is a contract between an investor and an insurance company, under which the investor make a lump-sum payment or series of payments. In return, the insurer agrees to make periodic payments to the investor beginning immediately or at some future date. Annuities typically offer tax-deferred growth (similar to a 401K or 403B plan) of earnings and may include a death benefit that will pay the investor's designated beneficiary a guaranteed minimum amount, such as the investor's total purchase payments.

---

93   http://www.sec.gov/answers/annuity.htm

There are generally two types of annuities—fixed and variable. In a fixed annuity, the insurance company guarantees the investor will earn a minimum rate of interest during the time that the account is growing. The insurance company also guarantees that the periodic payments will be a guaranteed amount per dollar in the account. These periodic payments may last for a definite period, such as 20 years, or an indefinite period, such as the investor's lifetime or the lifetime of the investor and his spouse.

In a variable annuity (similar to a variable whole life policy), by contrast, one can choose to invest the purchase payments among a range of different investment options, typically mutual funds. The rate of return on the purchase payments, and the amount of the periodic payments remitted to the investor, will vary depending on the performance of the investment options selected. The reason people would invest in variable annuities over fixed annuities would be for the opportunity to achieve a greater return, although the investor is assuming a greater degree of risk.

One type of variable annuity is an equity-indexed annuity. During the accumulation period, when the investor makes either a lump sum payment or a series of payments, the insurance company credits the investor with a return that is based on changes in a stock market equity index, such as the S&P 500 Index. The insurance company typically guarantees a minimum return. Guaranteed minimum return rates vary. After the accumulation period, the insurance company will make periodic payments to the investor under the terms of the contract, unless one chooses to receive the contract value in a lump sum.

Variable annuities are securities regulated by the SEC, and the investor must receive a **prospectus** outlining the security's investment objectives. Fixed annuities are not securities and are not regulated by the SEC, because they exclude an investment option. The payments are guaranteed as long as the insurance company does not go bankrupt (this was a huge concern during the sub-prime mortgage crisis). Equity-indexed annuities make payments that are linked to the performance of the underlying index, and combine features of traditional insurance products (guaranteed minimum return) and traditional securities. Depending on the mix of features, an equity-indexed annuity may or may not be a security. The typical equity-indexed annuity is not registered with the SEC.

REVERSE MORTGAGES

There is another income generating tool that is becoming increasingly popular with seniors. These are reverse mortgages. A reverse mortgage is a type of home loan that allows a homeowner to convert a portion of the equity in his or her home into cash. The equity built up over years of home mortgage payments can be paid to the homeowner. Unlike a traditional home equity loan or second mortgage, **no repayment is required until the borrower(s) no longer use the home as their principal residence.** The federal department of Housing and Urban Development's (HUD) reverse mortgage tool provides these benefits, and it is federally-insured as well[94]. To qualify for a reverse mortgage, one needs to meet the following qualifications:

- Be a homeowner, age 62 or older
- Own your home outright or have a mortgage balance that can be paid at closing with the proceeds of the reverse loan
- You must live in the home

A traditional second mortgage, or a home equity line of credit, requires you to have a sufficient income versus debt ratio to qualify for the loan, and you are required to make monthly mortgage payments. The reverse mortgage is different in that it pays you, and is available regardless of your current income. The amount you can borrow depends on your age, the current interest rate, and the appraised value of your home. Generally, the more valuable your home is, the older you are, and the lower the interest, the more you can borrow. You don't make payments, because the loan is not due as long as the house is your principal residence. Like all homeowners, you still are required to pay your real estate taxes and other conventional payments like utilities, but you cannot be foreclosed or forced to vacate your house because you "missed your mortgage payment[95]".

Before rushing out to apply for a reverse mortgage, homeowners should be aware that this type of loan has several downsides. Closing costs and fees can be steep, and if you are thinking about leaving your home in two to three

94   http://www.hud.gov/offices/hsg/sfh/hecm/rmtopten.cfm
95   Ibid

years, this is not a financially prudent way to extract money from your home. In that case, a home equity loan is likely a cheaper option[96]. In addition, most reverse mortgage products come with variable interest rates pegged to such short-term indexes such as the London Interbank Offered Rate (LIBOR), plus a margin. Interest is charged on the outstanding balance and accrues over time, increasing the loan amount. This is the magic of compounding interest at work in reverse – meaning it favors the lender instead of you.

ADVANCED DIRECTIVES / LIVING WILLS

I sometimes refer to estate planning as death preparation because it is the time in your life where certain decisions need to be made that, while unpleasant, can provide one with the peace of mind that comes from knowing that loved ones will be taken care of financially and that the respective government entities will have minimal involvement in the distribution of your life-long possessions. The preparation of an advance directive constitutes one of these unpleasant but necessary episodes. An advance directive tells your doctor what kind of care you would like to have if you become unable to make medical decisions (if you are in a coma, for example).[97] A good advance directive describes the kind of treatment you would want depending on how sick you are. For example, the directives would describe what kind of care you want if you have an illness that you are unlikely to recover from, or if you are permanently incapacitated and unable to make your own medical decisions.

96   http://seattlepi.nwsource.com/money/383881_real18.html
97   http://familydoctor.org/online/famdocen/home/pat-advocacy/endoflife/003.html

Advance directives usually tell your doctor that you don't want certain kinds of treatment. However, they can also say that you want a certain treatment no matter how ill you are.

A living will is an advanced directive that comes into play when an individual is terminally ill with usually six months or less of life remaining. Like an advanced directive, the document can describe the type of treatment you wish to receive in your final days. A durable power of attorney (DPA) for health care is another kind of advance directive. A DPA states that you have chosen to make health care decisions yourself. It becomes active any time you are unconscious or unable to make medical decisions. A DPA is generally more useful than a living will, but a DPA may not be a good choice if you do not have a person you trust to make these decisions for you.[98] Finally, a Do Not Resuscitate order (DNR) is another type of advanced directive which directs physicians and other healthcare providers not to perform any extraordinary efforts (no CPR) to keep you alive. In many cases, elderly people wish to die with dignity and prefer to avoid repetitive efforts to keep them alive, such as artificial breathing and other methods of life support.

<u>Summary / Tips to Remember</u>
- Wills are legal documents transferring wealth from the deceased to one's beneficiaries
- Probate is the legal proceeding providing the court's stamp of approval to said will
- Trusts are vehicles used with the primary objective of bypassing probate; two key types are *revocable* and

---

98   Ibid

irrevocable; the latter can often avoid punitive estate taxation.

- Insurance is the protection against personal and /or monetary loss:
    - Life – protects against loss of income – two key categories are *whole* life and *term* life
    - Medical – protection against medical injury – plans usually sold by employers and paid for through voluntary deductions
    - Automobile – protection against personal injury or damage to one's or another party's vehicle
    - Property / Casualty – protection against damage to one's dwelling or business as well as to oneself from some type of extraordinary event (tornado, fire, hurricane, theft, etc…)
- Annuities and Reverse mortgages offer retirees with alternatives to increase their monthly income streams; however, each of these will result in a decrease to the owner's net worth and asset base.

TAXES

Although taxes do not comprise one of the six major pillars of financial freedom, it is critical to have a basic understanding of all the different taxes Americans are responsible for. This allows households to plan accordingly and realize how much or how little disposable income they truly have. It is also critical for preventing surprises on tax day, April 15. Following is a general description of the major tax categories in the American lexicon.

FEDERAL INCOME TAXES

When most of us think of taxes, we immediately think of federal income taxes, which comprise the single largest tax most Americans pay each year. These taxes are calculated based on a percentage of a household's taxable income net of qualified deductions. This figure is the result of all sources of household income adjusted downward by contributions to tax-deferred accounts and a few ancillary items. The U.S. tax code that the Internal Revenue Service (IRS) employs is based on a system known as a *progressive income tax* using **marginal** tax rates. The percentage each household uses to calculate their tax obligation varies depending on what one's income bracket is. In 2010, six different tax brackets were in existence, reflecting marginal tax rates consistent with increasing household income levels. These tax brackets are set by the current administration (Republican or Democrat) in power with Congressional approval, but the income levels these percentages apply to vary based on whether the tax return is filed by a married couple filing a joint return, a single person, a married couple filing a separate return, a head of the household (think divorced or single parent), etc. Following is a chart reflecting current tax rate brackets by marital status.

Tax Bracket	Single	MFJ	MFS	HoH
10%	$ 8,375	$ 16,750	$ 8,375	$ 11,950
15%	$ 34,000	$ 68,000	$ 34,000	$ 45,550
25%	$ 82,400	$ 137,300	$ 82,400	$ 117,650
28%	$ 171,850	$ 209,250	$ 104,625	$ 190,550
33%	$ 373,650	$ 373,650	$ 186,825	$ 373,650
35%	> $373,650	> $373,650	> $186,825	> $373,650

http://taxes.about.com/od/preparingyourtaxes/a/tax-rates_2.htm

Marginal tax rates are the key to these bracket calculations. This implies that every dollar within each tax bracket is taxed at a particular rate. The first dollar of taxable income in excess of a particular bracket threshold will be taxed at the percentage corresponding to the next higher tax bracket. Following is a theoretical example for the Smith household assuming they file a joint tax return.

Taxable Income - $112,000
Married Filing Jointly

Tax Bracket	Bracket Limit	Tax
10%	$ 16,750	$ 1,675
15%	$ 68,000	$ 7,688
25%	$ 137,300	$ 11,000
Total		**$ 20,363**

The example shows the Smith's would owe $20,363 in federal income tax (18.2% of total taxable income). Once again, this figure is arrived at by multiplying the first $16,750 of income by 10 percent, yielding a subtotal of $1,675. The next $51,250 worth of income is multiplied by 15 percent for a subtotal of $7,688, which added to $1,605 yield a new subtotal of $9, 363. The final income portion of $44,000 is taxed at a rate of 25 percent, for a subtotal of $11,000, which is added to the previous sub-total of $9,363 for a total tax due of $20,363.

Obviously this is a steep figure to come up with all at once. Many individuals, especially if they work for corporations or smaller businesses, will have income **withheld** every pay period from their salary, which will be set aside for their annual tax obligation. The withholding amount will be determined based on several factors: a) the total income they generate in their particular job b) the amount of voluntary deductions taken for savings and medical plans and c) an assumption for certain deductions from income consistent with federal tax regulations.

Some individuals who do not work in firms which withhold part of their salary to pay federal income taxes may have to pay **estimated** taxes each quarter to the IRS based on their expected annual obligation. The common thread with these periodic tax payments is that the government wants to collect as much of the tax revenue in advance rather than wait for a lump sum at the end of the year. The tax code benefits married couples filing jointly over every other filing status. The government would like a society which encourages marriage and families. Married couples filing separately are subject to the most stringent tax burdens, as the government discourages divorce due to its impact on family unity. Were the Smith's to file "separately", they would have a higher tax burden placed on them:

Taxable Income - $112,000
Married Filing Separately

Tax Bracket	Bracket Limit		Tax	
10%	$	8,375	$	838
15%	$	34,000	$	3,844
25%	$	82,400	$	12,100
28%	$	104,625	$	6,223
33%	$	186,825	$	2,434
Total			$	25,438

This couple will wind up owing 22.7% of their total taxable household income in taxes merely by filing under a more onerous marital status. This results in an increase of $5,075 or 25% from the more generous "married filing jointly" status. **Moral of the story: sometimes divorce can be hazardous to your wallet!**

As you might imagine, the lower the taxable income, the lower the total tax obligation will be, and the lower the percentage of taxable income that will be paid in taxes. Each year, millions of homeowners file their personal income taxes using a process known as **itemizing**. This is in sharp contrast to the provision of a **standard deduction** which much of the population still uses, but which offers a lower deduction from taxable income than itemizing does, leading to higher income tax liabilities for the household. **The main objective of itemizing is to reduce the total taxable income as much as possible!!** The way to do this legally (tax avoidance vs. tax evasion) is to identify qualified deductions that reduce the total taxable income level. You will recall that in the Home Ownership chapter I referenced the tax advantage that owning a home offers compared to making monthly rent payments. The reason for this is that in the early years of home ownership, the mortgage payment consists primarily of interest obligations (see amortization chart in the Home Ownership chapter). *Mortgage interest is 100% tax deductible, whereas rent payments are not!* Following is a list of some of the major tax deductions present today in the IRS tax code:

- Home mortgage interest
- Charitable deductions (Church, Goodwill, Salvation Army, Purple Heart, etc...)

- Medical expenses greater than 7.5% of adjusted gross income
- IRA deductions
- Alimony paid
- State, local, and property taxes
- Un-reimbursed business costs (used primarily by independent contractors and small businesses under Schedule C)

Each year, millions of taxpayers try to record as many of these qualified expenses as possible on Form 1040 with the hopes of reducing their total taxable income and, in turn, reducing their total federal income tax obligation. Many people who choose to rent their primary residence will not have enough qualified deductions to itemize their tax return and will be allowed instead to use a standard deduction which will reduce the taxpayer's total taxable income. If the taxpayer has qualified deductions in excess of the standard deduction amount, it is always preferable for the homeowner to choose to **itemize** the tax return.

STATE INCOME TAXES

The state version of income taxes works in much the same way as federal taxes do. State taxes are calculated using varying percentages of a household's adjusted gross income, which tabulates all income sources for the household, "from whatever source derived". In addition, they are also **withheld** periodically from the taxpayer's salary. However, there are a couple of major differences. Certain states, such as Florida, Texas and Nevada, **charge no income tax at all.** And state tax rates typically are much smaller in percentage terms, ranging from 5% to 10%. Most states that impose income taxes on their residents also levy a local (county) tax fee. Many times this tax is calculated as a percentage of the state income tax obligation, and is often referred to as a "piggyback" tax because it is lumped on top of the state income tax burden. **This tax is deductible for federal income tax purposes if the owner itemizes**.

PROPERTY TAXES

These are taxes on personal and real property. They are usually imposed on primary residences or rental properties, but in some states they are also levied on items such as boats, automobiles, and other big-ticket items. This tax can be fairly onerous and is usually assessed based on the total acreage of the property and will be higher in municipalities that represent high-demand living locations. For automobiles, this tax is usually assessed based on the book value or the remaining value of the car. Much like income taxes, homeowners will make payments toward their annual or semiannual property tax obligation each month as part of their total mortgage payment. Remember from the PITI calculation in the home ownership chapter that the T is the property tax obligation. This amount, which is paid monthly, sits in **escrow** or in an account set up specifically to handle this payment until the municipality invoices the homeowner for the tax. Like state income taxes, these payments are deductible for federal income tax purposes if the owner itemizes.

CAPITAL GAINS / DIVIDEND TAXES

More than 50% of American households own some combination of stocks, bonds, and mutual funds. If you recall from the investment chapter, there are two principal ways of earning income with investments. The first is by selling a stock, bond, or mutual fund for more money than what was paid. The difference is called a **capital gain**. The second way to earn income is by receiving periodic payments. Many stockholders receive quarterly dividend distributions, while bondholders usually receive semi-annual coupon or interest payments. Each of these income streams is taxed, but in a different manner. Capital gains are treated as an investment if held more than one year and are taxed at a current rate in 2010 of 15%. If the asset is sold in less than one year, any profit generated is taxed as **ordinary income** and will depend on the tax bracket to which the individual belongs. Stock dividends or taxable bond interest earned (state municipal bond interest earned is usually tax-free at the federal level) is always taxed at the ordinary income rate. The difference in rates is rooted in the attempt to encourage long-term savings instead of short-term trading. You will notice the capital gain tax rate is significantly lower than the ordinary income rate in order to encourage long-term investment by the investing public.

PAYROLL TAXES

Every paycheck issued by organizations employing individuals includes non-tax-deductible, line item deductions for the purpose of funding Social Security, Medicare (which is discussed in greater detail in the nursing/long-term care chapter), and federal and state unemployment programs. Many details of these entitlement programs are also discussed in the Macro Economic overview. It is good to remember though that Social Security is a pay-as-you-go program, which means the government writes checks to today's beneficiaries using payroll taxes collected from today's workers. In 2010, Social Security will pay retirement and survivors benefits to more than 44 million Americans and disability benefits to another 10 million. Meanwhile, 156.6 million workers contributed to the program in 2010, resulting in a 2.9:1 worker to beneficiary ratio. This shrinking ratio is perhaps the biggest threat to the long term solvency of the program. Additional proof of this shrinking worker to beneficiary ratio is the fact that the number of Social Security beneficiaries is growing faster than the number of workers paying taxes to support them. **The number of elderly between now and 2041 are expected to increase by nearly 100%, while the total number of workers is expected to increase by a much smaller percentage leading to a projected worker to beneficiary ratio of only 2.1:1 in 30 years!!**

When Social Security began in 1935, the payroll tax on workers' salaries to support the program was 1 percent on the first $3,000 of income. Today, Social Security is financed by a 12.4 percent payroll tax—half by the employee and half by the employer—on the first $106,800 of income[99]. Please note that in 2011, the social security tax has been reduced to 8.4% for one year only (50% employee / employer) in order to stimulate a sluggish economy.

It is readily apparent that many of today's working Americans do not believe the program will be in place when

---

99   http://www.ssa.gov/pressoffice/factsheets/HowAreSocialSecurity.htm

they reach retirement age. For those on the lower end of the income scale, this is especially concerning: 54% of married retirees and 73% of single retirees depend on Social Security for more than 50% of their income; 22% of married seniors and 43% of single seniors rely on the program for more than 90% of their retirement income..

Adding to the problem is a greater life expectancy and a shrinking average household. In 1940, life expectancy was 61.4 for men and 65.7 for women. By 2000, life expectancy was 74.2 for men and 79.5 for women. By 2050, life expectancy will be 79.2 for men and 83.4 for women. People are also having fewer children. For each generation to be the same size as the one before (the replacement rate), women must have 2.1 children. In 1940, the fertility rate was 2.23. Today, the rate is 2.07, and by 2050 it is expected to trend downward to 1.95.

The bottom line to these statistics is that by 2015, Social Security is projected to spend more in benefits than it collects in taxes. By 2037, the program is expected to have spent all the assets credited to the trust fund, and taxes will have to rise by half or benefits will have to be cut by a third to make up the difference. It is estimated that between 2017 and 2076 (the end of the actuarial scoring period), Social Security's unfunded liability (the total of all the annual deficits) will be as much as $16 Trillion—more than 5 times the size of the 2010 federal budget![100]

---

100 http://www.heritage.org/research/reports/2010/08/2010-social-security-trustees-report-reform-needed-now

SALES AND USE TAXES

These are taxes collected on virtually all goods and services and are imposed by the merchant selling the item being purchased. The seller must then remit the tax proceeds to the proper state or local municipality. Most states impose sales taxes on individuals, but there are a few, like Delaware, that attract many cross-border customers by imposing **no sales taxes** on purchased items. At this point, there is no national sales tax imposed at the federal level, given that the federal government prefers the progressive income tax system to act as the main revenue generating source to fund its needs.

ESTATE TAXES

Few people have historically qualified for this tax, but if a household has amassed a sizeable net worth over one's lifetime, there is a good probability that one's estate may be taxed one final time upon death. The way it currently works is that if the total value of one's assets, less all corresponding liabilities, exceeds a specific amount, each dollar of taxable assets exceeding the specified amount is taxed by the federal government at a very high rate which has typically approached 50%. Assets include household possessions ranging from cash, investments, homes, business interests, artwork, net book value of automobiles, etc. Liabilities include outstanding loans, mortgage balances, credit card debt, and any other money owed by the estate at the time of death.

In 2001, a new tax law was passed that, among other things, included a provision which gradually decreased the tax liability to those estates which exceeded the $1M threshold, in place at the time the law was enacted. One item of note: When the principal owner of the estate passes away, he can bequeath the entire estate tax-free to the spouse. However, upon the death of the spouse, that individual's estate would then be liable for the taxes due on the total value of said estate, unless those assets were protected by a trust. Below is a table that was developed as a result of the 2001 tax law. It reflects the annual dollar amount at which the estate tax kicks in and the applicable tax rate affecting those dollars in excess of the taxable amount.[101]

Year	Applicable Exclusion Limit	Maximum tax rate
2002	$1 million	50%
2003	$1 million	49%
2004	$1.5 million	48%
2005	$1.5 million	47%
2006	$2 million	46%
2007	$2 million	45%
2008	$2 million	45%
2009	$3.5 million	45%
2010	Repeal of estate tax	35% (gift tax only)
2011	$1 million	55%

Source: U.S. Joint Committee on Taxation.

101 http://taxguru.org/estate/706.htm

As you can see, the law stipulates that the exclusion limit rises each year as the applicable tax rate declines. What this means is that fewer families will qualify for this tax in the future, and if they do qualify the actual tax will continue to decrease as a percentage of the total dollar amount in excess of the exclusion limit. This pattern continues until 2010, when the current law eliminates the estate tax altogether. However, in order to pass Congress, lawmakers had to include a sunset provision in this law which means that the estate tax was supposed to return to its original 2001 terms one year after elimination, or by 2011. **Recently, Congress declared a one year moratorium on the reinstatement of the estate tax, leaving the repeal in place through 2011.** This is a hotly contested issue in Congress and you can expect additional changes to this law as time moves on. In my opinion, the estate law, which only applies to about 2% of households, is extremely cruel. It penalizes a lifetime of achievement at such time the remaining spouse bequeaths the inheritance to the corresponding heirs.

GIFT TAXES

Proper estate planning should include gifts to heirs which aid in reducing the total value of the estate in question, thereby reducing the applicable tax should the value of the estate still exceed the thresholds reflected in the table in the previous section. The gift tax applies to the transfer by gift of any property. You make a gift if you give property (including money), without expecting to receive something of at least equal value in return. If you sell something at less than its full value or if you make an interest-free or reduced interest loan, you may be making a gift. The general rule is that any gift is a taxable gift. However, there are many exceptions to this rule. Generally, the following gifts are not taxable gifts.

- Gifts that are less than the annual exclusion for the calendar year
- Tuition or medical expenses you pay for someone (the educational and medical exclusions)
- Gifts to your spouse
- Gifts to a political organization for its use
- Gifts to qualified charities (A deduction is available for these amounts.)

A separate annual exclusion applies to each person to whom you make a gift. In 2010, the annual exclusion was $13,000[102]. Therefore, each spouse can give up to $13,000 to each child or donee and none of the gifts will be taxable to the donor or the donee. It is important to remember that gifts to individuals are *not deductible* on the donor's income tax returns.[103]

MISCELLANEOUS TAXES

The previous categories represent the vast majority of taxes individuals will be compelled to pay. However, this by no means represents all taxes Americans may have to pay. There are many hidden taxes contained within the various obligations the typical consumer faces each day. For example, at any given time a large percentage of the price per gallon

---

102 http://gifttaxexclusion.com/
103 http://www.irs.gov/businesses/small/article/0,,id=108139,00.
html#4

for gasoline in the U.S. is comprised of various federal, state, and environmental tax obligations.[104]

A typical phone bill will contain various taxes, fees and surcharges, some of which will be calculated as a percentage of your total bill, so the larger the base charges, the greater the tax payment required by the vendor. If you smoke or drink, you will undoubtedly pay significantly "sin" taxes on cigarettes and alcohol. If you have significant wealth and purchase a boat or expensive automobile, you may be liable for a "luxury" tax on your purchase, merely for being able to pay for an expensive good.

Taxes are a part of life. There is no way to eliminate all of them. However, a consumer can definitely take certain steps to avoid a higher tax burden than necessary by becoming aware of legal deductions when filing annual tax returns, as well as by knowing which states charge sales and use taxes as well as income taxes. In addition, the individual may decide to create certain trust vehicles to avoid estate taxes and other proactive measures aimed at reducing one's overall liability. I highly recommend that those Americans choosing to itemize their taxes perform a study at the end of each tax year that estimates their total obligation the following April when individual income tax returns are due.

Summary / Tips to Remember
- The American tax landscape comprises many different types of taxes, which in aggregate may consume

---

104 http://waystoconservegas.com/do-you-care-more-about-the-cost-of-gasoline-or-the-environmental-costs.html

as much as 50% of one's total household income, if not more in certain cases

- Tax avoidance is the art of interpreting the internal revenue service (IRS) tax code with the objective of mitigating one's tax exposure; tax evasion is avoiding one's legitimate tax liability
- The United States has a progressive income tax system; meaning, the more one earns in income, the greater the tax percentage at the *margin* (meaning in excess of certain income thresholds)
- When preparing a federal income tax return (1040) understanding the following schedules is essential:
  - Schedule A – Itemized Deductions – allows you to deduct qualified deduction such as a) Medical and Dental costs > 7.5% of Adjusted Gross Income (AGI) b) State and Local Income and Property taxes paid c) Mortgage Interest paid d) Charitable Contributions e) Other Miscellaneous itemized deductions that exceed 2.5% of AGI
  - Schedule B – Interest Income – need to file if interest income exceeds $400
  - Schedule C – Business income – allows one to report business income generated and associated costs that were not reimbursed
  - Schedule D – Investment Profit / Loss

CONCLUSION

Each one of these chapters has a common thread that unites them. They represent a personal finance umbrella spanning your entire adult life. Whether the discussion surrounds the preparation of a family budget to prioritize the household goals and objectives, how to properly determine how expensive a home you can afford, or understanding how to protect your accumulated assets through the purchase of the right amount of insurance, anticipation and planning are required in order to remain ahead of the curve. This is a never-ending process. Just when you feel like your household finances are right where you desire, a large unplanned expenditure can rear its ugly head. Whether you require a new roof on your home or a loved one becomes terminally ill, these can represent large financial drains on the family. No one has a crystal ball. Yet if you plan and save accordingly and set aside money for unexpected events, you will be in a much better position to handle them at such time as they occur.

If you only follow one or two of the recommendations mentioned throughout this book, I would urge that as a household, you instill the discipline to eliminate your consumer debt position. Credit card debt can become a slippery slope; even if you go into debt for a short period of time, it can be most difficult to extricate yourself. Financial freedom is one of the greatest gifts one can provide for their household. However, this does not necessarily equate to becoming financially wealthy. It merely refers to achieving a financial position which provides a household with the flexibility to do the things in life which lead to a greater degree of happiness and security. For some it might mean the ability to purchase an extra car. For others it means being able to afford to pay for your children's college education, weddings, or other big-ticket items. For others it could mean that one spouse has the option to remain at home to raise the children. A myriad of options are available if you manage to rid yourselves of the financial anchor that debt can become.

In addition, do yourself a huge favor and take advantage of any and all tax-deferred savings plans. Contribute the maximum amount possible to them and take advantage of any employer matching contributions within those plans. Remember that you are paying yourself first by contributing to these investment vehicles. No one is as interested in your financial position as much as you are. Finally, consult your investment advisor to ensure that your investments are suited to your risk tolerance.

ABOUT THE AUTHOR

You may ask yourself, just how successful is the author? I am by no means independently wealthy. My wife and I are both in our late thirties to early forties and we form a two-income household. Melanie and I both hold graduate degrees. Mine is in the field of finance, hers in the healthcare arena. I went to Loyola College in Baltimore, MD, for my undergraduate and graduate school education. Melanie went to Villa Julie College in Baltimore, MD, for her undergraduate studies in nursing, and completed her graduate work at the University of Maryland, School of Nursing.

We live in a comfortable home in Ellicott City, MD, and have no interest bearing credit card debt to our names. We have no current car loans. Our portfolios are growing, though not yet incredibly large, and we strive to contribute double-digit percentages of our income to our retirement accounts on a monthly basis, taking advantage of our employer matches. We have paid-up insurance policies that, while not conducive to early retirement for either one of us, will pay off the balance of the home mortgage should one of us suffer an untimely death. We have a will, which will safely transfer our entire net worth to our children. Long-term care planning is not on the horizon as of yet, but it is an obligation for which we plan to eventually prepare. Lastly, financial anxieties are not really present in our household. We would love to be independently wealthy, but we take solace in knowing that we are living slightly below our means, which allows us the flexibility to meet most financial hurdles that may be coming down the path. Most important, we both understand that the road to financial freedom is more like a marathon rather than a sprint.